# Anatomy & Physiology

# 1,160
# Multiple Choice Questions
## For Exam Success

By

Kate L Tierney

www.beautyandholisticstudies.com

## Copyright Information

The information contained in this document is the property of www.beautyandholisticstudies.com. No part of this document shall be duplicated, transmitted, resold, or reproduced in any form or by any means without prior written permission from www.beautyandholisticstudies.com.

If you have any information regarding the illegal re-selling or duplication of this document, please report the offending person to info@beautyandholisticstudies.com.

## Disclaimer

www.beautyandholisticstudies.com assumes no responsibility for the use, or misuse, of this product, or for any injury, damage, and/or financial loss sustained by persons or property as a result of using this report.

We cannot guarantee your future results and/or success as each case is personal and there may be unforeseen circumstances with an individual.

The use of this information should be based on your own due diligence and you agree that our company is not liable for any success or failure of your business that is directly or indirectly related to the purchase and use of this information.

# Introduction

This book is aimed at students studying towards Holistic or Beauty Qualifications. It has been designed as a revision resource, which should be used in conjunction with class text books.

There are 13 chapters, with a total of 1,160 Multiple Choice Questions. Each question has 4 possible answers, with an answer grid at the end of each chapter. You will also be able to practice for your exams by completing the 58 crosswords provided. With hundreds of clues covering all systems of the body, these puzzles are designed to be repeated several times until your confidence grows.

Anatomy & Physiology, 1,160 MCQ is considered to be one of the most popular and successful anatomy & physiology revision guides on the market today, having already assisted thousands of students worldwide in completing their exams with ease.

Test yourself daily with a mixture of questions. Do this regularly and you will find the subject of anatomy & physiology becoming a little easier to manage.

# Other Titles Available

Anatomy & Physiology Student Workbook – 2,000 Puzzles & Quizzes

Beauty Therapy Level 2 Revision Questions – 2,000 Multiple Choice Questions

Cosmetology Revision Questions – 3,000 Multiple Choice Questions

# Contents

# Chapter 1 | The Cell & Tissues

## Multiple Choice Questions

| | |
|---|---|
| **1. What does cytoplasm not contain?**<br>a) Mitochondria<br>b) Ribosomes<br>c) Nucleus<br>d) Endoplasmic reticulum<br><br>*Answer:* _____ | **2. What part of the cell allows the movement of substances from one cell to another?**<br>a) Nucleus<br>b) Vacuoles<br>c) Centrioles<br>d) Endoplasmic reticulum<br><br>*Answer:* _____ |
| **3. What is the centre of a cell called?**<br>a) Nucleus<br>b) Vacuoles<br>c) Nucleolus<br>d) Mitochondria<br><br>*Answer:* _____ | **4. A group of tissues join to form;**<br>a) Organ<br>b) System<br>c) Organism<br>d) Cells<br><br>*Answer:* _____ |
| **5. What is the first stage of mitosis?**<br>a) Anaphase<br>b) Prophase<br>c) Metaphase<br>d) Telophase<br><br>*Answer:* _____ | **6. Cuboidal epithelium is found in;**<br>a) Circulatory system<br>b) Kidneys<br>c) Lymph vessels<br>d) Stomach & Intestines<br><br>*Answer:* _____ |
| **7. The process where large complex substances are broken down into simple substances is called?**<br>a) Phagocytosis<br>b) Pinocytosis<br>c) Anabolism<br>d) Catabolism<br><br>*Answer:* _____ | **8. What is the smallest unit of matter?**<br>a) Molecule<br>b) Atom<br>c) Cell<br>d) Element<br><br><br><br>*Answer:* _____ |

| | |
|---|---|
| **9. Which type of tissue contains fibrocytes?**<br>a) Adipose<br>b) Lymphoid<br>c) Areolar<br>d) Bone<br><br>*Answer:* _____ | **10. Empty spaces within the cytoplasm are called;**<br>a) Vacuoles<br>b) Mitochondria<br>c) Endoplasmic reticulum<br>d) Golgi apparatus<br><br>*Answer:* _____ |
| **11. What is a cell mainly composed of?**<br>a) Cytoplasm<br>b) Centrioles<br>c) Water<br>d) Mitochondria<br><br>*Answer:* _____ | **12. Where is ATP produced?**<br>a) Nucleus<br>b) Nucleolus<br>c) Mitochondria<br>d) Ribosomes<br><br>*Answer:* _____ |
| **13. What is the function of non keratinised compound epithelium?**<br>a) To absorb shock<br>b) To provide lubrication<br>c) To prevent skin from drying out<br>d) To support simple epithelium<br><br>*Answer:* _____ | **14. 2 pairs of centrioles separate during which phase of mitosis?**<br>a) Prophase<br>b) Anaphase<br>c) Telophase<br>d) Metaphase<br><br>*Answer:* _____ |
| **15. DNA can be found in;**<br>a) Mitochondria<br>b) Cytoplasm<br>c) Nucleus<br>d) Golgi Apparatus<br><br>*Answer:* _____ | **16. A group of similar cells form;**<br>a) An organ<br>b) Tissue<br>c) Ligament<br>d) Nucleus<br><br>*Answer:* _____ |
| **17. Where in the cell is protein produced?**<br>a) Lysosomes<br>b) Ribosomes<br>c) Golgi apparatus<br>d) Mitochondria<br><br>*Answer:* _____ | **18. The spindle fibres disappear during which phase of mitosis?**<br>a) Metaphase<br>b) Prophase<br>c) Interphase<br>d) Telophase<br><br>*Answer:* _____ |

**19. Physiology refers to;**
a) The study of the body's structures
b) The study of the body's cells
c) The study of the functions of the body
d) The study of the form of the body

*Answer:* _____

**20. When 2 or more atoms join together they form?**
a) Tissue
b) Cell
c) Molecule
d) System

*Answer:* _____

**21. What is the most widely distributed connective tissue in the body?**
a) Adipose
b) Areolar
c) Yellow elastic
d) Lymphoid

*Answer:* _____

**22. What is the function of hyaline cartilage?**
a) Helps to maintain the shape of an area
b) Flexibility & support
c) To add nutrients to articulating surfaces
d) Stretch & recoil

*Answer:* _____

**23. What is the function of the nucleolus?**
a) The control the centre of the cell
b) To produce chromosomes
c) To produce protein
d) Form ribosomes

*Answer:* _____

**24. Where does the cell receive its energy from?**
a) Oxygen
b) Mitochondria
c) Centrosomes
d) Golgi apparatus

*Answer:* _____

**25. Human cells contain how many chromosomes?**
a) 46
b) 42
c) 33
d) 23

*Answer:* _____

**26. Which one of the following is not contained within protoplasm?**
a) Carbohydrates
b) Cytoplasm
c) Proteins
d) Lipids

*Answer:* _____

**27. The reproduction of a sex cell is called;**
a) Mitosis
b) Osmosis
c) Filtration
d) Meiosis

*Answer:* _____

**28. The power houses of a cell are known as;**
a) Lysosomes
b) Centrioles
c) Nucleus
d) Mitochondria

*Answer:* _____

| | |
|---|---|
| **29. What organelle breaks down food, making it easier to digest?**<br>a) Vacuoles<br>b) Nucleolus<br>c) Ribosomes<br>d) Lysosomes<br><br><br>*Answer:* _____ | **30. Define centrioles;**<br>a) Dense areas of cytoplasm<br>b) Pairs of cylindrical structures, usually at right angles next to each other<br>c) The point where 2 chromatids join in the chromosome<br>d) Gaps within the cytoplasm<br><br>*Answer:* _____ |
| **31. At the metaphase of mitosis;**<br>a) The centriole divides into 2 centromeres<br>b) Spindle threads of the centrioles separate to form 2 chromosomes<br>c) The cell is resting<br>d) The chromosomes align themselves at the centre of the cell and eventually each chromosome replicates<br><br>*Answer:* _____ | **32. What is the energy transporting molecule produced by mitochondria?**<br>a) ATP<br>b) Oxygen<br>c) Protoplasm<br>d) Cytoplasm<br><br><br><br>*Answer:* _____ |
| **33. How many chromosomes are in a sex cell before fertilisation?**<br>a) 46<br>b) 52<br>c) 23<br>d) 17<br><br><br>*Answer:* _____ | **34. What type of tissue is adipose tissue?**<br>a) Nervous tissue<br>b) Permeable tissue<br>c) Elastic tissue<br>d) Fatty tissue<br><br><br>*Answer:* _____ |
| **35. Ciliated epithelium is found in;**<br>a) Endocrine system<br>b) Circulatory system<br>c) Digestive system<br>d) Respiratory system<br><br><br>*Answer:* _____ | **36. What is formed when the zygote divides?**<br>a) Foetus<br>b) Embryo<br>c) Ovum<br>d) Gamete<br><br><br>*Answer:* _____ |

| | |
|---|---|
| **37. What process of metabolism releases energy?**<br>a) Catabolism<br>b) Homeostasis<br>c) Phagocytosis<br>d) Anabolism<br><br>*Answer:* _____ | **38. The study of the structure of the body is known as;**<br>a) Histology<br>b) Homeostasis<br>c) Physiology<br>d) Anatomy<br><br>*Answer:* _____ |
| **39. Which part of the cell regulates what substances enter and leave a cell?**<br>a) Cytoplasm<br>b) Nucleur membrane<br>c) Nucleus<br>d) Cell membrane<br><br><br><br><br>*Answer:* _____ | **40. What is the process called whereby small molecules, like oxygen and carbon dioxide, can pass through the cell membrane?**<br>a) Diffusion<br>b) Osmosis<br>c) Filtration<br>d) Dissolution<br><br>*Answer:* _____ |
| **41. Cell reproduction is known as?**<br>a) Osmosis<br>b) Diffusion<br>c) Meiosis<br>d) Mitosis<br><br><br><br>*Answer:* _____ | **42. An area of cytoplasm which contains the centrioles is called;**<br>a) Chromatid<br>b) Centromere<br>c) Chromosome<br>d) Centrosome<br><br><br>*Answer:* _____ |
| **43. Squamous epithelium is found in;**<br>a) Kidney tubules<br>b) Lymphatic tissue<br>c) Lining of the heart, blood and lymph vessels<br>d) Lining of the bladder<br><br><br><br><br>*Answer:* _____ | **44 What is the function of the cell membrane?**<br>a) To control every organelle within the cytoplasm<br>b) To destroy harmful parts of a cell<br>c) To hold the organelles within the cell<br>d) To let carbohydrates pass through the cell<br><br>*Answer:* _____ |

**45. Osmosis describes;**
a) The process of moving small molecules such as oxygen and carbon dioxide through the cell membrane
b) The process of moving water through the cell membrane from an area of high concentration to an area of low concentration or vice versa
c) The movement of water across a membrane
d) The transfer of glucose and amino acids through the cell membrane to equal concentration

Answer: _____

**46. What is the function of areolar tissue?**
a) Protection and elasticity
b) To reduce heat loss
c) To connect and support
d) To provide attachment

Answer: _____

**47. Which one of the following is a process of metabolism?**
a) Anabolism
b) Organelle
c) Cytoplasm
d) Golgi Apparatus

Answer: _____

**48. Phagocytosis describes;**
a) The process used by cells to engulf and destroy harmful bacteria
b) The process used by cells to absorb nutrients and other substances
c) The process by which cells obtain energy by osmosis
d) The process by which nutrients are released from a cell

Answer: _____

**49. What is the second phase of mitosis?**
a) Metaphase
b) Telophase
c) Prophase
d) Interphase

Answer: _____

**50. How many chromosomes does a zygote have?**
a) 46
b) 12
c) 23
d) 32

Answer: _____

**51. The golgi apparatus is responsible for;**
a) Circulation
b) Energy production
c) Digestion
d) Communication

Answer: _____

**52. The transport of substances in a cell is helped by;**
a) Ribosomes
b) Mitochondria
c) Endoplasmic Reticulum
d) Lysosomes

Answer: _____

| 53. Stratified epithelium is a type of; | 54. Function of yellow elastic cartilage; |
|---|---|
| a) Compound epithelial tissue<br>b) Simple epithelial tissue<br>c) Ciliated epithelial tissue<br>d) Transitional epithelial tissue<br><br>*Answer:* _____ | a) Connection<br>b) Protection<br>c) Flexibility<br>d) Insulation<br><br>*Answer:* _____ |
| **55. Non keratinised stratified epithelium can be found;**<br>a) Lining of the mouth<br>b) Lining of large intestine<br>c) Liver<br>d) Hair, skin & nails<br><br>*Answer:* _____ | **56. What is protoplasm?**<br>a) A network of membranes that forms a system of sacs<br>b) A small body within the nucleus<br>c) The centre of the cell<br>d) A translucent substance that makes up a cell<br><br>*Answer:* _____ |
| **57. A group of systems join to form;**<br>a) An organ<br>b) Tissue<br>c) An organism<br>d) Cells<br><br>*Answer:* _____ | **58. In which phase of mitosis does the nucleolus disappear?**<br>a) Interphase<br>b) Telophase<br>c) Prophase<br>d) Anaphase<br><br>*Answer:* _____ |
| **59. The point where 2 identical chromatids come into contact in the chromosome is called;**<br>a) Centrosome<br>b) Centriole<br>c) Centromere<br>d) Nucleus<br><br>*Answer:* _____ | **60. The study of cells and tissue is called;**<br>a) Histology<br>b) Physiology<br>c) Homeostasis<br>d) Meiosis<br><br>*Answer:* _____ |
| **61. What is the function of adipose tissue?**<br>a) Secretory<br>b) Protective<br>c) Recoil<br>d) Connecting<br><br>*Answer:* _____ | **62. Which type of cartilage is found in the intervertebral discs?**<br>a) Adipose<br>b) Yellow elastic<br>c) Hyaline<br>d) White fibrocartilage<br><br>*Answer:* _____ |

| | |
|---|---|
| **63. What is the process of metabolism that consumes energy?**<br>a) Phagocytosis<br>b) Anabolism<br>c) Catabolism<br>d) Respiration<br><br>*Answer:* _____ | **64. What is an atom?**<br>a) The smallest unit of matter<br>b) The largest unit of matter<br>c) The simplest substance in the body<br>d) The structure of a cell<br><br><br><br>*Answer:* _____ |
| **65. What is the function of endoplasmic reticulum?**<br>a) To transport substances from one part of a cell to another<br>b) Growth and repair<br>c) Destroys worn out parts of a cell<br>d) Secretes carbohydrates<br><br>*Answer:* _____ | **66. What part of the cell stores and transports the protein out of the cell?**<br>a) Ribosomes<br>b) Mitochondria<br>c) Golgi apparatus<br>d) Nucleus<br><br><br><br>*Answer:* _____ |
| **67. What substance forms chromosomes?**<br>a) Centrosomes<br>b) Centrioles<br>c) Centromere<br>d) Chromatin<br><br><br><br>*Answer:* _____ | **68. Which one of the following is a function of the nucleus?**<br>a) To secrete waste materials and transport them out of the cell membrane<br>b) To control the cell's functions<br>c) To form the circulation of a cell<br>d) Cell reproduction<br><br>*Answer:* _____ |
| **69. What organ does adipose tissue protect?**<br>a) Kidneys<br>b) Heart<br>c) Nose<br>d) Lungs<br><br>*Answer:* _____ | **70. Where are goblet cells found?**<br>a) Columnar epithelium<br>b) Squamous epithelium<br>c) Compound epithelium<br>d) Cuboidal epithelium<br><br><br>*Answer:* _____ |

| | |
|---|---|
| **71. What is the function of the centrioles?**<br>a) Supply the centrioles with energy<br>b) Store waste materials for transport outside the cell<br>c) Centrioles are involved in cell reproduction<br>d) Circulation of oxygen around the cell<br><br>*Answer: _____* | **72. What is the largest organelle?**<br>a) Nucleus<br>b) Mitochondria<br>c) Ribosome<br>d) Cell body<br><br><br><br><br><br>*Answer: _____* |
| **73. What do groups of molecules form?**<br>a) Atoms<br>b) Cells<br>c) Tissue<br>d) Organs<br><br><br><br><br>*Answer: _____* | **74. Metabolism describes;**<br>a) The physiological processes of the cell<br>b) The physiological processes of the body<br>c) The physiological processes of the tissues<br>d) The psychological processes of the body<br><br>*Answer: _____* |
| **75. What is the function of vacuoles?**<br>a) Growth and repair<br>b) Storage<br>c) Energy<br>d) Circulation<br><br>*Answer: _____* | **76. Lymphoid tissue is a type of;**<br>a) Muscular tissue<br>b) Nervous tissue<br>c) Ciliated tissue<br>d) Connective tissue<br><br>*Answer: _____* |
| **77. Keratinised stratified epithelium can be found;**<br>a) Lining of the oesophagus<br>b) Hair, skin and nails<br>c) Inside mouth<br>d) Lining of the bladder<br><br>*Answer: _____* | **78. Which type of cartilage is found on the surfaces of joints?**<br>a) Hyaline<br>b) Yellow elastic<br>c) Elastic<br>d) White fibrocartilage<br><br>*Answer: _____* |
| **79. A group of organs join to form;**<br>a) Tissue<br>b) A system<br>c) An organ<br>d) An organism<br><br>*Answer: _____* | **80. Which type of epithelium lines the bladder?**<br>a) Stratified<br>b) Transitional<br>c) Ciliated<br>d) Simple<br><br>*Answer: _____* |

| | |
|---|---|
| **81. What is the structure of the cell membrane?**<br>a) A semi permeable membrane, made of protein and fats<br>b) A semi permeable membrane, made of fats and carbohydrates<br>c) A semi permeable membrane, made of water and tissue<br>d) A semi permeable membrane, made of water and protein<br><br>*Answer: _____* | **82. During the interphase of mitosis;**<br>a) A new nuclear membrane appears<br>b) The cell is resting<br>c) The nucleolus disappears<br>d) The centromere divides into 2 centrosomes<br><br>*Answer: _____* |
| **83. What is the fourth stage of mitosis?**<br>a) Telophase<br>b) Interphase<br>c) Prophase<br>d) Anaphase<br><br>*Answer: _____* | **84. What is the function of lysosomes?**<br>a) Storage<br>b) Aid digestion<br>c) Destroy worn out parts of a cell, bacteria and any unwanted substances<br>d) Formation of ATP<br><br>*Answer: _____* |
| **85. What is the function of white fibrocartilage?**<br>a) To connect joints<br>b) To maintain an organ<br>c) To provide heat<br>d) To absorb shock<br><br>*Answer: _____* | **86. Which type of connective tissue is able to stretch and alter its shape?**<br>a) Areolar<br>b) Adipose<br>c) Yellow elastic<br>d) White fibrous<br><br>*Answer: _____* |
| **87. The process by which living cells absorb liquids;**<br>a) Catabolism<br>b) Phagocytosis<br>c) Pinocytosis<br>d) Metabolism<br><br>*Answer: _____* | **88. An example of a molecule;**<br>a) Oxygen<br>b) Carbon<br>c) Hydrogen<br>d) Carbon Dioxide<br><br>*Answer: _____* |
| **89. Where is lymphoid tissue found?**<br>a) Lining of the stomach<br>b) Heart lining<br>c) The appendix<br>d) The respiratory system<br><br>*Answer: _____* | **90. What is the third phase of mitosis?**<br>a) Interphase<br>b) Metaphase<br>c) Anaphase<br>d) Telophase<br><br>*Answer: _____* |

| 91. What is the function of white fibrous tissue? | 92. What is the function of ribosomes? |
|---|---|
| a) Insulatory | a) To supply the cell with energy |
| b) Stretching | b) To allow movement of substances throughout the cell |
| c) Supports organs | c) To produce protein |
| d) Protecting and supporting surrounding structures | d) Control the cell |
| *Answer:* _____ | *Answer:* _____ |
| 93. Which type of tissue protects and supports? | 94. At the anaphase of mitosis the; |
| a) Connective | a) The centrioles separate and form spindle fibres |
| b) Muscular | b) Identical pairs of chromosomes move to one end of the cell and the other pairs move to the opposite end of the cell |
| c) Nervous | c) Centrosome divides into 2 centrioles |
| d) Epithelium | d) Cell is resting |
| *Answer:* _____ | *Answer:* _____ |
| 95. Anabolism describes; | 96. Which one of the following is an example of an atom? |
| a) The minimum energy required to keep the body going | a) Hydrogen |
| b) The process of engulfing foreign particles | b) $H_2O$ |
| c) The process of building up complex substances from simple molecules | c) Carbon Dioxide |
| d) The process of storing energy | d) Organ |
| *Answer:* _____ | *Answer:* _____ |

# The Cell – Crossword 1

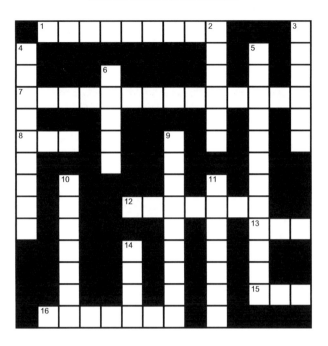

## Across

1. In what phase of mitosis does the spindle fibres disappear and the cell divides to form 2 cells? (9)
7. Proteins that are not used in the cell are transported out of the cell by what? (14)
8. What kind of cell is a gamete? (3)
12. What is used for the growth and repair of a cell? (7)
13. What part of a cell contains the genetic material to make a human? (3)
15. What is the main energy transporter within the cell? (3)
16. Transferring water through the membrane to maintain equilibrium on both sides (7)

## Down

2. What does mitochondria supply the cell with? (6)
3. What do a group of cells join together to form? (6)
4. What type of enzymes do lysosomes contain?
5. Power houses of the cell (12)
6. What stage of mitosis is prophase? (5)
9. The protein factories of a cell (9)
10. Cell division (7)
11. What is the cell doing during the interphase? (7)
14. Lipids (4)

# The Cell – Crossword 2

## Across
1. What part of the cell is used for storage, transport and digestion? (8)
3. What does white fibrocartilage absorb? (5)
8. A group of organs join to form what? (6)
10. Non keratinised stratified compound epithelium (3)
11. What is the most general connective tissue found on the body?
12. What phase of mitosis is the anaphase? (5)
13. What type of cartilage is found on the ends of bones which form joints? (7)
14. What controls the cell's functions? (7)

## Down
2. Fatty tissue (7)
4. What is the most common type of tissue in the body? (10)
5. During what stage of mitosis are chromosomes formed? (8)
6. The study of cells and tissues (9)
7. Paired, rod shaped structures contained within the centrosomes (10)
9. What are vacuoles used for? (7)

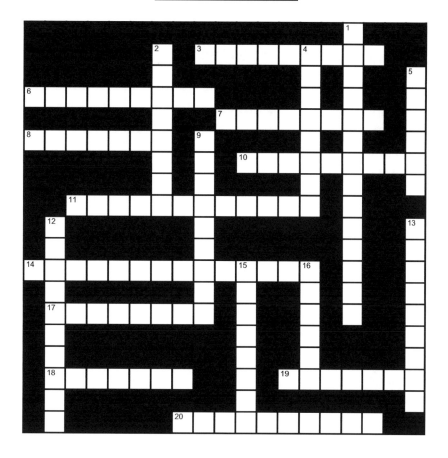

**Across**

3. A process by which substances are transferred through the cell membrane (9)

6. Part of the cell containing enzymes that digest bacteria and destroy unwanted substances (9)

7. What type of simple epithelium carries mucus and unwanted substances away from the lungs, keeping the passageways clear? (8)

8. A function of yellow elastic tissue (7)

10. Strands of uncoiled DNA (9)

11. Type of cells found in cartilage (12)

14. Which part of the cell stores the protein produced by the endoplasmic reticulum? (14)

17. What do a group of systems join to form? (8)

18. Fatty tissue (7)

19. Tissue found in the brain and spinal cord (7)

20. At what stage does the cell prepare itself for cell division? (10)

**Down**

1. A type of stratified compound epithelium found on the conjunctiva of the eyes (14)
2. A type of connective tissue (8)
4. Epithelium found lining the heart and blood vessels (8)
5. What stage of mitosis is the metaphase? (6)
9. A gel like substance containing organelles (9)
12. The entire contents of the cells including the nucleus and cytoplasm (10)
13. Stage of mitosis where the chromosomes align themselves at the centre of the cell (9)
15. Third phase of mitosis (8)
16. A type of epithelium (6)

# The Cell - Crossword 4

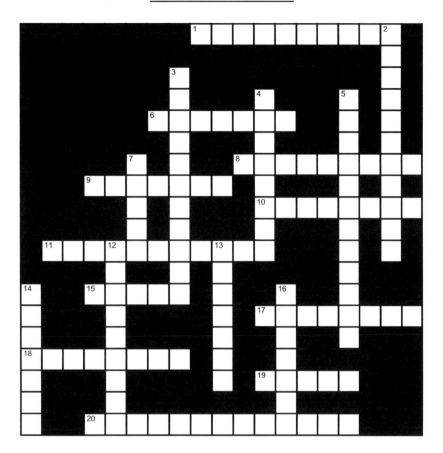

**Across**

1. A type of compound epithelium (10)
6. What type of connective tissue is found in almost all parts of the body? (7)
8. A small, dense area within the nucleus (9)
9. What type of cartilage is smooth and has a bluish white appearance? (7)
10. What type of tissue contains lymphocytes? (8)
11. Areas of clear cytoplasm near the nucleus (11)
15. A type of connective tissue containing erythrocytes, thrombocytes and leucocytes (5)
17. Epithelium which consists of a single layer of cube shaped cells (8)
18. Which phase of mitosis does the chromatin shorten and thicken to form chromosomes? (8)
19. What does a chromosome carry? (5)
20. What type of cartilage contains elastic fibres? (13)

**Down**

2. The process by which a solid or liquid forms a solution in a solvent (11)
3. Stratified epithelium that prevents the cells in the deeper layers from drying out (11)
4. Empty spaces within the cytoplasm (8)
5. Where in the cell is ATP produced? (12)
7. Which substance makes up the majority of a cell? (5)
12. Fourth stage of mitosis (9)
13. Reproduction of a sex cell (7)
14. A connective tissue which helps to protect organs (7)
16. Part of the cell which controls the cell's growth and repair (7)

## Multiple Choice Answers – The Cell & Tissues

| | | | | | | | | | | |
|---|---|---|---|---|---|---|---|---|---|---|
| 1 | C | 21 | B | 41 | D | 61 | B | 81 | A |
| 2 | D | 22 | B | 42 | D | 62 | D | 82 | B |
| 3 | A | 23 | D | 43 | C | 63 | B | 83 | A |
| 4 | A | 24 | B | 44 | C | 64 | A | 84 | C |
| 5 | B | 25 | A | 45 | B | 65 | A | 85 | D |
| 6 | B | 26 | B | 46 | C | 66 | C | 86 | C |
| 7 | D | 27 | D | 47 | A | 67 | D | 87 | C |
| 8 | B | 28 | D | 48 | A | 68 | B | 88 | D |
| 9 | C | 29 | D | 49 | A | 69 | A | 89 | C |
| 10 | A | 30 | B | 50 | A | 70 | A | 90 | C |
| 11 | C | 31 | D | 51 | D | 71 | C | 91 | D |
| 12 | C | 32 | A | 52 | C | 72 | A | 92 | C |
| 13 | B | 33 | C | 53 | A | 73 | B | 93 | A |
| 14 | A | 34 | D | 54 | C | 74 | B | 94 | B |
| 15 | C | 35 | D | 55 | A | 75 | B | 95 | C |
| 16 | B | 36 | B | 56 | D | 76 | D | 96 | A |
| 17 | B | 37 | A | 57 | C | 77 | B | | |
| 18 | D | 38 | D | 58 | C | 78 | A | | |
| 19 | C | 39 | D | 59 | C | 79 | B | | |
| 20 | C | 40 | A | 60 | A | 80 | B | | |

## Crossword Answers – The Cell & Tissues

### Crossword 1

**Across**
1. Telophase
7. Golgi Apparatus
8. Sex
12. Protein
13. DNA
15. ATP
16. Osmosis

**Down**
2. Energy
3. Tissue
4. Digestive
5. Mitochondria
6. First
9. Ribosomes
10. Mitosis
11. Resting
14. Fats

### Crossword 2

**Across**
1. Vacuoles
3. Shock
8. System
10. Wet
11. Areolar
12. Third
13. Hyaline
14. Nucleus

**Down**
2. Adipose
4. Connective
5. Prophase
6. Histology
7. Centrioles
9. Storage

## Crossword 3

**Across**
3. Diffusion
6. Lysosomes
7. Ciliated
8. Stretch
10. Chromatin
11. Chondrocytes
14. Golgi Apparatus
17. Organism
18. Adipose
19. Nervous
20. Interphase

**Down**
1. Non Keratinised
2. Lymphoid
4. Squamous
5. Second
9. Cytoplasm
12. Protoplasm
13. Metaphase
15. Anaphase
16. Simple

## Crossword 4

**Across**
1. Stratified
6. Areolar
8. Nucleolus
9. Hyaline
10. Lymphoid
11. Centrosomes
15. Blood
17. Cuboidal
18. Prophase
19. Genes
20. Yellow Elastic

**Down**
2. Dissolution
3. Keratinised
4. Vacuoles
5. Mitochondria
7. Water
12. Telophase
13. Meiosis
14. Adipose
16. Nucleus

# Chapter 2 | The Skin, Hair & Nails

## Multiple Choice Questions

| | |
|---|---|
| **1. What is the visible part of the cuticle called?**<br>a) Eponychium<br>b) Mantle<br>c) Hyponychium<br>d) Matrix<br><br>*Answer:* _____ | **2. Leukonychia describes;**<br>a) Cracking of the skin around the nail plate<br>b) White spots on the nail<br>c) Flaking nails<br>d) Forward growth of the cuticle<br><br>*Answer:* _____ |
| **3. Desquamation can be defined as;**<br>a) The dead skin cells on the surface of the skin are constantly shedding<br>b) Granules which are visible in healing after trauma<br>c) A pigmentation which gives skin its colour<br>d) Cell division<br><br>*Answer:* _____ | **4. How is melanin produced?**<br>a) By cells called melanocytes<br>b) During the process of desquamation<br>c) In the sweat glands of the dermis<br>d) By cells called histiocytes<br><br><br><br>*Answer:* _____ |
| **5. What part of the nail lies at the base of the nail under the eponychium?**<br>a) Matrix<br>b) Mantle<br>c) Peronychium<br>d) Nail plate<br><br>*Answer:* _____ | **6. Onychatrophia describes;**<br>a) The nail becoming smaller<br>b) Forward growth of the cuticle<br>c) White spots on the nail bed<br>d) Lifting of the nail plate<br><br><br>*Answer:* _____ |
| **7. Erector pili can be defined as;**<br>a) Hair follicles which produce sebum<br>b) Small muscles which are attached to each hair follicle<br>c) Microscopic capillaries<br>d) Nerve endings<br><br>*Answer:* _____ | **8. Which one of the following cannot be absorbed by the skin?**<br>a) Drugs<br>b) Water<br>c) Almond oil<br>d) Essential oils<br><br><br>*Answer:* _____ |

| | |
|---|---|
| **9. Where is terminal hair found?**<br>a) On a foetus<br>b) Eyebrows<br>c) Eyelids<br>d) Soles of the feet<br><br>*Answer:* _____ | **10. What can cause hang nails?**<br>a) Illness<br>b) Dry cuticles<br>c) Age<br>d) Nail biting<br><br>*Answer:* _____ |
| **11. Which skin disorder affects the forehead, cheeks and nose, causing a flushed reddened appearance?**<br>a) Acne vulgaris<br>b) Eczema<br>c) Herpes zoster<br>d) Acne rosacea<br><br>*Answer:* _____ | **12. What skin condition is the result of having no melanocytes?**<br>a) Papilloma<br>b) Albinism<br>c) Vitiligo<br>d) Naevae<br><br><br><br>*Answer:* _____ |
| **13. Which one of the following is the protective outer layer of the hair?**<br>a) Outer root sheath<br>b) Medulla<br>c) Cuticle<br>d) Cortex<br><br>*Answer:* _____ | **14. Inflammation of the tissue surrounding the nails is called;**<br>a) Onychia<br>b) Onycholysis<br>c) Onychorrhexis<br>d) Paronychia<br><br>*Answer:* _____ |
| **15. How would you recognise onychomycosis?**<br>a) Yellow or white patches at the free edge which may spread and grow towards the root<br>b) The free edge splits and peels into several layers<br>c) A red swollen area surrounding the nail, pus may be present<br>d) White spots on the nail plate<br><br>*Answer:* _____ | **16. Which one of the following is the resting stage of hair growth?**<br>a) Anagen<br>b) Interphase<br>c) Catagen<br>d) Telogen<br><br><br><br><br><br><br><br><br>*Answer:* _____ |
| **17. Comedones are also known as;**<br>a) Freckles<br>b) Hives<br>c) Blackheads<br>d) Whiteheads<br><br>*Answer:* _____ | **18. The stratum lucidum is known as;**<br>a) Clear layer<br>b) Surface layer<br>c) Basal layer<br>d) Granular layer<br><br>*Answer:* _____ |

**19. What is a carbuncle?**
a) An infection of the skin caused by highly contagious blisters
b) A dark patch of pigmentation on the face
c) An overgrowth of tissue on a freckle
d) An infection of a group of hair follicles

Answer: _____

**20. Spoon shaped nails are referred to as;**
a) Pterygium
b) Onychauxis
c) Onychophagy
d) Koilonychia

Answer: _____

**21. Which pigment gives skin its natural colour?**
a) Histamine
b) Melanin
c) Heparin
d) Collagen

Answer: _____

**22. What is the purpose of collagen in the skin?**
a) To repair the skin
b) To reduce redness
c) To produce the anticoagulant heparin
d) To keep the skin firm and elastic

Answer: _____

**23. Where does nail growth occur?**
a) Eponychium
b) Mantle
c) Nail bed
d) Matrix

Answer: _____

**24. Lifting or separation of the nail from its bed is known as?**
a) Leuconychia
b) Onychophagy
c) Onycholysis
d) Onychia

Answer: _____

**25. The Acid Mantle is formed from;**
a) Eccrine & apocrine fluid
b) Mast cells
c) Sweat & sebum
d) Histamine & heparin

Answer: _____

**26. The body temperature of healthy humans is?**
a) 36.8 degrees celsius
b) 38.6 degrees celsius
c) 37.5 degrees celsius
d) 37.8 degrees celsius

Answer: _____

**27. What part of the hair lies above the skin's surface?**
a) Root
b) Bulb
c) Shaft
d) Matrix

Answer: _____

**28. Onychocryptosis is usually caused by;**
a) Nervous disorder
b) Ill fitting shoes
c) Illness
d) Age

Answer: _____

| | |
|---|---|
| **29. What substance in the skin is converted into Vitamin D from UV rays?**<br>a) Melanin<br>b) MSH<br>c) 7-dehydrocholesterol<br>d) Heparin<br><br>*Answer:* _____ | **30. Which of the following is a congenital skin disorder?**<br>a) Acne vulgaris<br>b) Psoriasis<br>c) Chloasma<br>d) Papilloma<br><br>*Answer:* _____ |
| **31. Which one of the following can be a cause of koilonychia?**<br>a) Biting the nail<br>b) Age<br>c) Iron deficiency<br>d) Trauma to the nail<br><br>*Answer:* _____ | **32. What part of the hair protects the cortex?**<br>a) Cuticle<br>b) Medulla<br>c) Matrix<br>d) Shaft<br><br>*Answer:* _____ |
| **33. Which of the following can be found in the epidermis?**<br>a) Sweat glands<br>b) Lymph vessels<br>c) Melanocytes<br>d) Elastin<br><br>*Answer:* _____ | **34. What type of skin disorder is impetigo?**<br>a) Viral infection<br>b) Congenital infection<br>c) Bacterial infection<br>d) General infection<br><br>*Answer:* _____ |
| **35. An overgrown cuticle which grows forward onto the nail plate is known as;**<br>a) Pterygium<br>b) Koilonychia<br>c) Paronychia<br>d) Onycholysis<br><br>*Answer:* _____ | **36. Infestation of lice on the head is known as;**<br>a) Pediculosis corporis<br>b) Pediculosis pubis<br>c) Pediculosis capitis<br>d) Pediculosis pedis<br><br>*Answer:* _____ |
| **37. Warts can be recognised by;**<br>a) Blocked glands<br>b) Horny papules, commonly found on the hands<br>c) Small pigmented areas of skin<br>d) Brown patches on the skin<br><br>*Answer:* _____ | **38. Ephelides are more commonly referred to as;**<br>a) Liver spots<br>b) Whiteheads<br>c) Blackheads<br>d) Freckles<br><br>*Answer:* _____ |

**39. Which one of the following is not a type of hair growth?**
a) Vellus
b) Lanugo
c) Terminal
d) Catagen

Answer: _____

**40. What is the cuticle skin found directly under the free edge?**
a) Proximal nail fold
b) Eponychium
c) Hyponychium
d) Perionychium

Answer: _____

**41. Which layer of the skin consists of dead skin cells?**
a) Stratum granulosum
b) Stratum spinosum
c) Stratum corneum
d) Stratum lucidum

Answer: _____

**42. Which type of tissue is the dermis made of?**
a) Elastic tissue
b) Fibrous tissue
c) Connective tissue
d) Muscular tissue

Answer: _____

**43. What causes a habit tic?**
a) By an individual constantly biting their nails
b) By an individual picking the cuticle area
c) By an individual constantly rubbing the surface of the nail plate
d) By an individual constantly picking the tissue surrounding the nail

Answer: _____

**44. Which one of the following is not found on the nail bed?**
a) Lymph vessels
b) Blood vessels
c) Nerves
d) Sebaceous glands

Answer: _____

**45. Blue nails may be caused by;**
a) Illness
b) Dark nail polish
c) Cigarettes
d) Poor circulation

Answer: _____

**46. Onychophagy describes;**
a) Egg shell nails
b) Hang nails
c) Ringworm
d) Bitten nails

Answer: _____

**47. What do Mast Cells produce?**
a) Areolar tissue
b) Histamine & heparin
c) Melanin
d) Red blood cells

Answer: _____

**48. What do Eccrine glands excrete?**
a) Milky fluid
b) Oil
c) Sebum
d) Watery sweat

Answer: _____

**49. What part of the nail forms a watertight seal between the free edge and the skin of the fingertip?**

a) Hyponychium

b) Perionychium

c) Matrix

d) Nail grooves

Answer: _____

**50. Which one of the following is the middle layer of the hair?**

a) Cortex

b) Shaft

c) Medulla

d) Bulb

Answer: _____

**51. Which one of the following is a viral infection?**

a) Verrucas

b) Lentigo

c) Milia

d) Psoriasis

Answer: _____

**52. Shingles is also known as;**

a) Urticaria

b) Herpes simplex

c) Chloasma

d) Herpes zoster

Answer: _____

**53. What part of the nail is made up of dead translucent layers of keratinised cells?**

a) Nail plate

b) Nail bed

c) Nail grooves

d) Proximal nail folds

Answer: _____

**54. Which one of the following is a layer of the hair?**

a) Cortex

b) Matrix

c) Dermal papillae

d) Keratin

Answer: _____

**55. Ringworm can also be referred to as;**

a) Herpes zoster

b) Tinea corporis

c) Tinea pedis

d) Dermatitis

Answer: _____

**56. What type of skin disorder is a port wine stain?**

a) Bacterial

b) Fungal

c) Viral

d) Pigmentation

Answer: _____

**57. What layer of the hair is responsible for determining the colour and sheen of the hair?**

a) Follicle

b) Cortex

c) Medulla

d) Cuticle

Answer: _____

**58. What is the mantle?**

a) The growing area of the nail

b) Deep fold of epidermis just before the cuticle at the base of the nail

c) The section of skin that the nail plate rests on

d) The grooves at the sides of the nail bed

Answer: _____

**59. What is dermatitis?**
a) An inflammation of the skin caused by contact with external factors
b) An allergy marked by the eruption of wheals with severe itching
c) An erythema covered with silvery scales
d) Eczema

Answer: _____

**60. Desquamation occurs on which layer of the skin?**
a) Stratum spinosum
b) Stratum lucidum
c) Granular layer
d) Stratum corneum

Answer: _____

**61. Where is vellus hair found?**
a) Face
b) Lips
c) Palms of the hands
d) Soles of the feet

Answer: _____

**62. Which one of the following is not an appendage of the skin?**
a) Sebaceous glands
b) Nails
c) Sweat glands
d) Sensory nerves

Answer: _____

**63. In which layer of the epidermis does mitosis occur?**
a) Prickle cell layer
b) Granular layer
c) Basal layer
d) Clear layer

Answer: _____

**64. A bacterial infection of the hair follicle is known as;**
a) Impetigo
b) Folliculitis
c) Dermatitis
d) Naevae

Answer: _____

**65. What is the function of the nail plate?**
a) To protect the nail mantle
b) To protect the matrix from damage
c) To provide blood supply to the nail bed
d) To protect the nail bed

Answer: _____

**66. What type of hair is fine and soft and is found on a foetus?**
a) Terminal
b) Lanugo
c) Vellus
d) Cuticle

Answer: _____

**67. Which one of the following is not a pigmentation disorder?**
a) Chloasma
b) Ephelides
c) Lentigo
d) Urticaria

Answer: _____

**68. A non malignant group of pigmented cells;**
a) Mole
b) Naevae
c) Urticaria
d) Chloasma

Answer: _____

| | |
|---|---|
| **69. Whitlow is also known as;**<br>a) Paronychia<br>b) Koilonychia<br>c) Pterygium<br>d) Onychophagy<br><br><br><br><br>*Answer:* _____ | **70. When does the inner root sheath stop growing?**<br>a) When it is level with the dermal papilla<br>b) When it is level with the sebaceous gland<br>c) When it is level with the matrix<br>d) When it is level with the outer root sheath<br><br>*Answer:* _____ |
| **71. Milia are more commonly referred to as;**<br>a) Whiteheads<br>b) Moles<br>c) Freckles<br>d) Blackheads<br><br>*Answer:* _____ | **72. The top layer of the epidermis is known as;**<br>a) Stratum lucidum<br>b) Stratum corneum<br>c) Stratum spinosum<br>d) Stratum germinativum<br><br>*Answer:* _____ |
| **73. Which one of the following sheaths is not part of the hair follicle?**<br>a) Inner root<br>b) Matrix<br>c) Outer root<br>d) Connective tissue<br><br>*Answer:* _____ | **74. The proximal nail fold is also known as;**<br>a) Mantle<br>b) Cuticle<br>c) Eponychium<br>d) Matrix<br><br><br>*Answer:* _____ |
| **75. Which layer of skin consists of living and dying cells?**<br>a) Basal layer<br>b) Prickle cell layer<br>c) Clear layer<br>d) Granular layer<br><br>*Answer:* _____ | **76. Which of the following cells are not found within the dermis?**<br>a) Leucocytes<br>b) Mast cells<br>c) Thrombocytes<br>d) Histiocytes<br><br>*Answer:* _____ |

| | |
|---|---|
| **77. Which hair type is longer and coarse?**<br>a) Lanugo<br>b) Catagen<br>c) Vellus<br>d) Terminal<br><br><br><br>*Answer:* _____ | **78. How would you recognize paronychia?**<br>a) Swollen, inflamed red skin around the nail, pus may be present<br>b) Small patches of red skin at the base of the nail, with silvery scales<br>c) Large areas of white or yellow patches on the nail<br>d) Grooves in the nail plate running from the base of the nail to the free edge<br><br>*Answer:* _____ |
| **79. Which one of the following is a contagious fungal infection?**<br>a) Onycholysis<br>b) Onychatrophia<br>c) Onychomycosis<br>d) Onychorrhexis<br><br>*Answer:* _____ | **80. What is the function of the lateral nail folds?**<br>a) To protect the base of the nail<br>b) To protect the proximal nail folds<br>c) To protect the mantle<br>d) To protect the edges of the nails<br><br>*Answer:* _____ |
| **81. Where is Sebum produced?**<br>a) Sebaceous glands<br>b) Apocrine glands<br>c) Lymphatic capillaries<br>d) Erector pili<br><br><br><br><br><br><br>*Answer:* _____ | **82. Hyperaemia can be defined as;**<br>a) A reduction in the blood's ability to carry oxygen<br>b) An increase of blood flow in the body causing the skin to become hot and flush<br>c) When the body becomes cold, body hair stands on end, raising the body temperature<br>d) When sweat and sebum form a protective barrier on the skin<br><br>*Answer:* _____ |
| **83. Where is the lunula located on the nail?**<br>a) Free edge<br>b) Base<br>c) Under the matrix<br>d) Side folds<br><br>*Answer:* _____ | **84. What is the thickest layer of the hair?**<br>a) Lanugo<br>b) Cortex<br>c) Medulla<br>d) Vellus<br><br><br><br>*Answer:* _____ |

**85. Eczema can be recognised by;**

a) Scaly red patches of skin that are itchy and dry

b) Yellow patches of skin

c) Red patches covered with silvery scales that are constantly shed

d) A pigmentation involving the upper cheeks

*Answer:* _____

**86. What type of skin disorder is Tinea Pedis?**

a) Fungal

b) Viral

c) Bacterial

d) Pigmentation

*Answer:* _____

**87. What is the active growing phase of the hair?**

a) Catagen

b) Anagen

c) Telogen

d) Vellus

*Answer:* _____

**88. What is the function of the eponychium?**

a) To provide the nail plate with nutrients

b) To produce new nail cells

c) To allow the nails to grow straight

d) To protect the matrix from infection

*Answer:* _____

**89. Malignant melanoma is defined as;**

a) A malignancy found in melanin

b) A malignant mole

c) A malignancy found in ergosterol

d) A tumour characterized by the cancerous growth of melanocytes

*Answer:* _____

**90. The Granular layer is known as;**

a) Stratum corneum

b) Stratum spinosum

c) Stratum granulosum

d) Stratum germinativum

*Answer:* _____

**91. What are the folds of skin overlapping the sides of the nail plate called?**

a) Peronychium

b) Nail grooves

c) Nail walls

d) Cuticle

*Answer:* _____

**92. Where is the connective tissue sheath positioned?**

a) It surrounds the sebaceous gland and follicle

b) It surrounds the outer root sheath

c) It grows from the base of the follicle

d) It grows from the lower section of the medulla

*Answer:* _____

**93. Which type of cells are responsible for the formation of collagen and elastic fibres?**
a) Fibroblasts
b) Mast cells
c) Leucocytes
d) Histiocytes

*Answer:* _____

**94. Which one of the following is not a function on the acid mantle?**
a) Keeps the skin moisturised
b) Protects the skin from harmful bacteria
c) Prevents infections
d) Controls temperature levels

*Answer:* _____

**95. What is the half moon of the nail called?**
a) Lunula
b) Matrix
c) Mantle
d) Free edge

*Answer:* _____

**96. What part of the hair follicle forms the follicle wall?**
a) Inner root sheath
b) Dermal papilla
c) Outer root sheath
d) Connective tissue sheath

*Answer:* _____

**97. A complete loss of colour on parts of the skin is known as?**
a) Vitiligo
b) Chloasma
c) Papilloma
d) Albinism

*Answer:* _____

**98. Liver spots are also known as;**
a) Vitiligo
b) Lentigo
c) Ephelides
d) Naevae

*Answer:* _____

**99. At what stage of hair growth does a new hair begin to grow in the hair follicle while the old hair sheds?**
a) Telogen
b) Catagen
c) Topical
d) Anagen

*Answer:* _____

**100. What is the free edge of a nail?**
a) The part of the nail plate that extends beyond the nail bed
b) The area where living cells are produced
c) The half moon shaped crescent at the base of the nail
d) The overlapping skin at the sides of the nails

*Answer:* _____

| | |
|---|---|
| **101. What part of the nail is a continuation of the matrix?**<br>a) Nail plate<br>b) Nail bed<br>c) Cuticle<br>d) Eponychium<br><br>*Answer:* _____ | **102. Ringworm is also known as;**<br>a) Onychorrhexis<br>b) Onychomycosis<br>c) Onychogryphosis<br>d) Onycholysis<br><br><br>*Answer:* _____ |
| **103. Chloasma can be recognised by;**<br>a) A complete lack of melanocytes<br>b) Small pigmented areas of the skin<br>c) Butterfly mask<br>d) A large area of dilated capillaries<br><br><br>*Answer:* _____ | **104. Sebum which becomes trapped in the base of a hair follicle with no surface opening causes;**<br>a) Blackheads<br>b) Whiteheads<br>c) Dermatitis<br>d) Acne rosacea<br><br>*Answer:* _____ |
| **105. The overlapping epidermis that surrounds the base of the nail is known as;**<br>a) Lunula<br>b) Cuticle<br>c) Nail walls<br>d) Nail grooves<br><br>*Answer:* _____ | **106. Which one of the following is the inner layer of the hair?**<br>a) Cuticle<br>b) Medulla<br>c) Keratin<br>d) Cortex<br><br><br><br>*Answer:* _____ |
| **107. The prickle cell layer of the skin is known as?**<br>a) Stratum spinosum<br>b) Stratum granulosum<br>c) Stratum lucidum<br>d) Stratum corneum<br><br>*Answer:* _____ | **108. Where are eccrine sweat glands found?**<br>a) Groin<br>b) Armpits<br>c) Nipples<br>d) All over the body<br><br><br>*Answer:* _____ |
| **109. What type of hair does not have a medulla?**<br>a) Vellus<br>b) Matrix<br>c) Lanugo<br>d) Terminal<br><br>*Answer:* _____ | **110. Which one of the following is commonly a bacterial infection?**<br>a) Paronychia<br>b) Onychomycosis<br>c) Pterygium<br>d) Onychophagy<br><br>*Answer:* _____ |

| | |
|---|---|
| **111. Which one of the following is not a bacterial skin disorder?**<br>a) Acne vulgaris<br>b) Boils<br>c) Impetigo<br>d) Verruca<br><br><br>*Answer:* _____ | **112. Tinea pedis can be recognised by;**<br>a) A small horny tumour found on the skin<br>b) Red patches on the skin covered with silvery scales<br>c) Flaking, scaling, itchy areas of skin between the toes<br>d) A lack of melanocytes<br><br>*Answer:* _____ |
| **113. What part of the follicle provides its nerve and blood supply?**<br>a) Hair bulb<br>b) Outer root sheath<br>c) Inner root sheath<br>d) Connective tissue sheath<br><br>*Answer:* _____ | **114. What is the function of the proximal nail folds?**<br>a) To protect the root of the nail<br>b) To protect the sides of the nail<br>c) To protect the free edge<br>d) To protect the nail bed<br><br>*Answer:* _____ |
| **115. A birth mark is known as;**<br>a) Port wine stain<br>b) Naevae<br>c) Chloasma<br>d) Vitiligo<br><br><br><br>*Answer:* _____ | **116. Redness of the skin, itching and erythema are common symptoms of which skin disorder;**<br>a) Herpes simplex<br>b) Chloasma<br>c) Papilloma<br>d) Dermatitis<br><br>*Answer:* _____ |
| **117. The perionychium describes;**<br>a) The extension of the nail plate beyond the nail bed<br>b) The skin that adheres to the base of the nail<br>c) The cuticles that overlap the sides of the nail<br>d) The deep fold of skin at the base of the nail<br><br>*Answer:* _____ | **118. What layer of the hair contains air spaces which cause the light to reflect off the hair?**<br>a) Cortex<br>b) Bulb<br>c) Catagen<br>d) Medulla<br><br><br><br><br><br>*Answer:* _____ |

**119. What is the term used to describe ingrown nails?**

a) Onychocryptosis

b) Onychomycosis

c) Onychophagy

d) Lamella dystrophy

Answer: _____

**120. What can cause leukonychia?**

a) Trauma to the matrix or the nail plate

b) Lifting of the nail plate

c) Ill fitting shoes

d) Ridges in the nail

Answer: _____

**121. The stratum germinativum is also known as?**

a) The granular layer

b) The basal layer

c) The clear layer

d) The surface layer

Answer: _____

**122. What is the PH balance of the skin?**

a) 5.5 - 6.5

b) 5.6 - 6.6

c) 4.5 - 5.6

d) 5.5 - 6.6

Answer: _____

**123. What is the term used to describe when the cuticle cracks and a small piece of skin protrudes at the side?**

a) Hang nail

b) Onychophagy

c) Leukonychia

d) Paronychia

Answer: _____

**124. What part of the nail does the nail plate rest on?**

a) Mantle

b) Matrix

c) Nail bed

d) Free edge

Answer: _____

**125. Infection of a hair follicle causing inflammation is known as?**

a) Herpes simplex

b) Boils

c) Folliculitis

d) Herpes zoster

Answer: _____

**126. Lentigo can be recognised by?**

a) Slightly raised brown patches of pigmentation

b) Small pigmented areas of skin

c) Large area of dilated capillaries

d) A complete loss of colour in large areas of the skin

Answer: _____

**127. Where in the hair does mitosis take place?**

a) Matrix

b) Medulla

c) Inner root sheath

d) Cortex

Answer: _____

**128. What is the function of the nail walls?**

a) To protect the sides of the nail plate

b) To protect the base of the nail plate

c) To provide nourishment to the nail bed

d) To protect the nail bed from infection

Answer: _____

**129. The clear layer of the epidermis;**
a) Stratum germinativum
b) Stratum lucidum
c) Stratum spinosum
d) Stratum corneum

Answer: _____

**130. Which one of the following is not a function of the skin?**
a) Absorption
b) Elimination
c) Sensation
d) Movement

Answer: _____

**131. What part of the nail keeps it growing forward in a straight line?**
a) Hyponychium
b) Nail folds
c) Nail grooves
d) Matrix

Answer: _____

**132. What is the enlarged part at the base of the hair root?**
a) Matrix
b) Bulb
c) Cuticle
d) Shaft

Answer: _____

**133. What protein is the nail plate made up of?**
a) Melanin
b) Rennin
c) Keratin
d) Trysin

Answer: _____

**134. What part of the nail protects and nourishes the nail?**
a) Nail mantle
b) Nail bed
c) Perionychium
d) Free edge

Answer: _____

**135. When the skin becomes too warm it automatically cools itself down. What is this process called?**
a) Vasodilation
b) Heat regulation
c) Vasoconstriction
d) Absorption

Answer: _____

**136. Which of the following skin disorders is contagious?**
a) Impetigo
b) Acne vulgaris
c) Chloasma
d) Comedones

Answer: _____

**137. Which one of the following gives the hair its strength?**
a) Catagen
b) Cuticle
c) Cortex
d) Medulla

Answer: _____

**138. Approximately how long does it take for the fingernail to grow from the cuticle to the free edge?**
a) 12 months
b) 6 months
c) 9 months
d) 3 months

Answer: _____

**139. What type of skin disorder do broken capillaries fall under?**

a) Bacterial

b) General

c) Pigmentation

d) Viral

Answer: _____

**140. Which layer of the skin contains melanocytes?**

a) Stratum granulosum

b) Stratum spinosum

c) Stratum corneum

d) Stratum germinativum

Answer: _____

**141. Where on the body is terminal hair not found?**

a) Scalp

b) Under the arms

c) Lips

d) Legs

Answer: _____

**142. Which one of the following nail diseases describes the thickening of the nail plate?**

a) Onychocryptosis

b) Onychauxis

c) Pterygium

d) Onychophagy

Answer: _____

**143. Tinea pedis is commonly referred to as;**

a) Ringworm

b) Athlete's foot

c) Cold sore

d) Shingles

Answer: _____

**144. Papilloma are more commonly referred to as;**

a) Freckles

b) Blackheads

c) Moles

d) Liver Spots

Answer: _____

**145. How would you recognize onychia?**

a) White spots on the nail plate

b) Inflammation of the nail bed which may be red and contain pus

c) White or yellow patches on the nail bed

d) Forward growth of the cuticle

Answer: _____

**146. What is the main part of the nail that we can see?**

a) Cuticle

b) Mantle

c) Nail folds

d) Nail plate

Answer: _____

**147. What layer of the hair contains melanin?**

a) Cuticle

b) Medulla

c) Vellus

d) Cortex

Answer: _____

**148. Horizontal, transverse furrows in the nail plate are known as?**

a) Claw nails

b) Beau's lines

c) Hang nails

d) Bruised nails

Answer: _____

| | |
|---|---|
| **149. Which one of the following is not a general skin disorder?**<br>a) Acne vulgaris<br>b) Dermatitis<br>c) Crows feet<br>d) Comedones<br><br>*Answer:* _____ | **150. Urticaria is also known as;**<br>a) Butterfly mask<br>b) Nettle rash<br>c) Cold sore<br>d) Shingles<br><br>*Answer:* _____ |
| **151. Onychocryptosis occurs when;**<br>a) The cuticle grows forward and becomes infected<br>b) The nail plate lifts from the nail bed<br>c) The nail is bitten too much<br>d) The side of the nail plate pushes into the lateral sidewalls<br><br>*Answer:* _____ | **152. At what stage of hair growth does the hair separate from the dermal papilla?**<br>a) Anaphase<br>b) Telogen<br>c) Catagen<br>d) Anagen<br><br>*Answer:* _____ |
| **153. A cold sore is also known as;**<br>a) Herpes zoster<br>b) Impetigo<br>c) Herpes simplex<br>d) Acne vulgaris<br><br>*Answer:* _____ | **154. When the skin is too cold it begins to heat itself up. What is this process called?**<br>a) Hyperaemia<br>b) Vasodilation<br>c) Heat regulation<br>d) Vasoconstriction<br><br>*Answer:* _____ |
| **155. How are cells in the nail hardened?**<br>a) By the process of phagocytosis<br>b) By the process of keratinisation<br>c) By the process of ossification<br>d) By the process of histology<br><br>*Answer:* _____ | **156. What protein is found in the hair?**<br>a) Lipase<br>b) Keratin<br>c) Melanin<br>d) Sebum<br><br>*Answer:* _____ |
| **157. Where are new nail cells produced?**<br>a) Nail plate<br>b) Eponychium<br>c) Mantle<br>d) Matrix<br><br>*Answer:* _____ | **158. Onychogryphosis describes;**<br>a) Ingrown toe nail<br>b) Flat or concave nail plate<br>c) Bitten nails<br>d) Very thick nail plate with an increased curve<br><br>*Answer:* _____ |

| | |
|---|---|
| **159. Flaking of the nail is known as;**<br><br>a) Onychomycosis<br>b) Koilonychia<br>c) Lamella dystrophy<br>d) Onychophagy<br><br><br>*Answer:* _____ | **160. What layer of hair gives it its elasticity?**<br><br>a) Medulla<br>b) Cortex<br>c) Sebaceous glands<br>d) Cuticle<br><br>*Answer:* _____ |
| **161. What part of the nail acts as a matrix seal and protects it from infection?**<br>a) Lunula<br>b) Cuticle<br>c) Nail grooves<br>d) Nail bed<br><br>*Answer:* _____ | **162. What part of the nail protects the matrix from physical damage?**<br>a) The free edge<br>b) The matrix<br>c) Nail mantle<br>d) The nail grooves<br><br><br><br>*Answer:* _____ |
| **163. Where is the inner root sheath located?**<br>a) At the base of the follicle at the dermal papilla<br>b) Surrounding the sebaceous gland<br>c) At the base of the hair root<br>d) Surround the erector pili muscle<br><br>*Answer:* _____ | |

# The Skin - Crossword 1

## Across

4. Shedding of the skin (12)
6. Freckles (9)
8. Whiteheads (5)
11. What effect does vasodilation have on the skin? (7)
13. Small benign tumours found on the skin, normally the hands (5)
14. What type of sweat do eccrine sweat glands excrete? (6)
16. Sweat glands producing milky fluid (8)
17. Stratum germinativum (10)

## Down

1. Liver spots (7)
2. Highly contagious weeping blisters (8)
3. Papilloma (4)
5. Bacterial infection (4)
7. Prickle cell layer (8)
9. What type of sweat do apocrine glands excrete? (5)
10. A pigment which gives skin its colour (7)
12. Pigmentation disorder (6)
15. What type of infection is a verruca? (5)

# The Skin - Crossword 2

**Across**

1. Fine lines around the eyes (9)
7. Cells within the dermis which produce histamine (11)
9. What substance in the dermis plumps up the skin? (8)
11. A complete loss of colour on areas of the skin (8)
12. Infection around a hair follicle (4)
13. Inflammatory skin disease with red, dry, itchy patches covered with silvery scales (9)
15. Blackhead (8)

**Down**

2. Bacterial infection of the hair follicle (12)
3. A pigmentation disorder that may be flat or raised, varying in size and colour (5)
4. Cells that produce collagen and elastin (11)
5. Area where sebaceous glands are not found (4)
6. Cells within the dermis that secrete histamine (4)
8. Function of the skin involved with sebum production (5)
10. What is produced by sebaceous glands? (5)
14. Colour of port wine stain (3)

# The Skin – Crossword 3

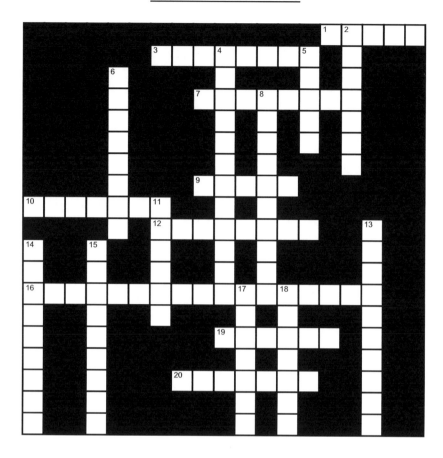

**Across**

1. The skin's natural moisturiser (5)
3. Tinea corporis (8)
7. Small areas of pigmented skin (8)
9. What substance can the skin mostly not absorb? (5)
10. What is produced by melanocytes? (7)
12. A pigmentation disorder (8)
16. A dangerous skin growth in a mole (17)
19. Inflammation of the skin with itchiness and dryness (6)
20. What supplies the hair with nourishment? (7)

**Down**

2. What gives skin its elasticity? (7)

4. Deepest layer of the epidermis (12)

5. Commonly found on dry skin (5)

6. What is required for the maintenance of healthy bones? (8)

8. A skin disorder which could be inherited (10)

11. Birth mark (6)

13. New cells are formed in what layer of the skin? (10)

14. What does a build up of sebum and waste in the hair follicles cause? (9)

15. The outermost layer of the skin (9)

17. A sweat gland (7)

18. What type of connective tissue is the papillary layer of the dermis made of? (7)

# The Skin - Crossword 4

**Across**

3. A small muscle attached to the hair follicle (11)

5. Increased areas of pigmentation, usually occurring on the face (8)

7. The process whereby dead skin cells are continually being shed (12)

11. Cells within the dermis (11)

12. What type of cells secrete collagen proteins? (11)

14. A wart found on the soles of the feet (7)

15. Bacterial infection (8)

17. What substance protects the deeper layers of the skin from UV light? (7)

18. What type of spot is a lentigo? (5)

19. Inflammatory condition of the skin (10)

20. Vasoconstriction (7)

**Down**

1. The innermost layer of the skin (6)
2. Basal layer (12)
4. Thick, red, itchy areas of skin with silvery scales (9)
6. Broken capillaries are generally found on what skin type? (9)
8. What type of infection is folliculitis? (9)
9. What does sweat and sebum on the surface of the skin form? (10)
10. Shingles (12)
13. Sweat glands found in the armpits (8)
16. Outermost layer of the epidermis (7)

## Multiple Choice Answers – The Skin, Hair & Nails

| # | Ans | | # | Ans | | # | Ans | | # | Ans | | # | Ans | | # | Ans |
|---|---|---|---|---|---|---|---|---|---|---|---|---|---|---|---|---|
| 1 | A | | 31 | C | | 61 | A | | 91 | C | | 121 | B | | 151 | D |
| 2 | B | | 32 | A | | 62 | D | | 92 | A | | 122 | C | | 152 | C |
| 3 | A | | 33 | C | | 63 | C | | 93 | A | | 123 | A | | 153 | C |
| 4 | A | | 34 | C | | 64 | B | | 94 | D | | 124 | C | | 154 | D |
| 5 | A | | 35 | A | | 65 | D | | 95 | A | | 125 | B | | 155 | B |
| 6 | A | | 36 | C | | 66 | B | | 96 | C | | 126 | A | | 156 | B |
| 7 | B | | 37 | B | | 67 | D | | 97 | A | | 127 | A | | 157 | D |
| 8 | B | | 38 | D | | 68 | A | | 98 | B | | 128 | A | | 158 | D |
| 9 | B | | 39 | D | | 69 | A | | 99 | A | | 129 | B | | 159 | C |
| 10 | B | | 40 | C | | 70 | B | | 100 | A | | 130 | D | | 160 | D |
| 11 | D | | 41 | C | | 71 | A | | 101 | B | | 131 | C | | 161 | B |
| 12 | B | | 42 | C | | 72 | B | | 102 | B | | 132 | B | | 162 | C |
| 13 | C | | 43 | C | | 73 | B | | 103 | C | | 133 | C | | 163 | A |
| 14 | D | | 44 | D | | 74 | A | | 104 | B | | 134 | B | | | |
| 15 | A | | 45 | D | | 75 | D | | 105 | B | | 135 | A | | | |
| 16 | D | | 46 | D | | 76 | C | | 106 | B | | 136 | A | | | |
| 17 | C | | 47 | B | | 77 | D | | 107 | A | | 137 | C | | | |
| 18 | A | | 48 | D | | 78 | A | | 108 | D | | 138 | B | | | |
| 19 | D | | 49 | A | | 79 | C | | 109 | C | | 139 | B | | | |
| 20 | D | | 50 | A | | 80 | D | | 110 | A | | 140 | D | | | |
| 21 | B | | 51 | A | | 81 | A | | 111 | D | | 141 | C | | | |
| 22 | D | | 52 | D | | 82 | B | | 112 | C | | 142 | B | | | |
| 23 | D | | 53 | A | | 83 | B | | 113 | D | | 143 | B | | | |
| 24 | C | | 54 | A | | 84 | B | | 114 | A | | 144 | C | | | |
| 25 | C | | 55 | B | | 85 | A | | 115 | B | | 145 | B | | | |
| 26 | A | | 56 | D | | 86 | A | | 116 | D | | 146 | D | | | |
| 27 | C | | 57 | C | | 87 | B | | 117 | C | | 147 | D | | | |
| 28 | B | | 58 | B | | 88 | D | | 118 | D | | 148 | B | | | |
| 29 | C | | 59 | A | | 89 | D | | 119 | A | | 149 | A | | | |
| 30 | B | | 60 | D | | 90 | C | | 120 | A | | 150 | B | | | |

## Crossword Answers – The Skin, Hair & Nails

### Crossword 1

**Across**
4. Desquamation
6. Ephelides
8. Milia
11. Cooling
13. Warts
14. Watery
16. Apocrine
17. Basal Layer

**Down**
1. Lentigo
2. Impetigo
3. Mole
5. Boil
7. Spinosum
9. Milky
10. Melanin
12. Naevae
15. Viral

### Crossword 2

**Across**
1. Crowsfeet
7. Histiocytes
9. Collagen
11. Vitiligo
12. Boil
13. Psoriasis
15. Comedone

**Down**
2. Folliculitis
3. Moles
4. Fibroblasts
5. Feet
6. Mast
8. Secretion
10. Sebum
14. Red

### Crossword 3

**Across**
1. Sebum
3. Ringworm
7. Freckles
9. Water
10. Melanin
12. Albinism
16. Malignant Melanoma
19. Eczema
20. Papilla

**Down**
2. Elastin
4. Germinativum
5. Milia
6. Vitamin D
8. Congenital
11. Naevae
13. Basal Layer
14. Comedones
15. Epidermis
17. Eccrine
18. Areolar

### Crossword 4

**Across**
3. Erector Pili
5. Chloasma
7. Desquamation
11. Histiocytes
12. Fibroblasts
14. Verruca
15. Impetigo
17. Melanin
18. Liver
19. Dermatitis
20. Warming

**Down**
1. Dermis
2. Germinativum
4. Psoriasis
6. Sensitive
8. Bacterial
9. Acid Mantle
10. Herpes Zoster
13. Apocrine
16. Corneum

# Chapter 3 | The Skeletal System

## Multiple Choice Questions

**1. What parts of the body does the appendicular skeleton support?**
a) Shoulder girdle, the upper limbs, the pelvic girdle and lower limbs
b) Torso
c) Head, neck and torso
d) Shoulder girdle and pelvic girdle

*Answer:* _____

**2. Which one of the following is an example of a long bone?**
a) Carpals
b) Ribs
c) Ethmoid
d) Phalanges

*Answer:* _____

**3. The scapula falls under which category of bone?**
a) Irregular bone
b) Flat bone
c) Short bone
d) Sesamoid bone

*Answer:* _____

**4. Which one of the following is not a function of the skeleton?**
a) Protection
b) Support
c) Heat absorption
d) Movement

*Answer:* _____

**5. Haversian canals can be defined as;**
a) Small channels running lengthways
b) Small channels running lengthways through compact bone
c) Small channels running lengthways through cancellous bone
d) Small channels found in cancellous bone containing oxygen and nutrients

*Answer:* _____

**6. Which bones form the bridge of the nose?**
a) Ethmoid bones
b) Nasal bones
c) Vomer
d) Lacrimal

*Answer:* _____

**7. What anatomical direction describes above or towards the upper part?**
a) External
b) Lateral
c) Distal
d) Superior

*Answer:* _____

**8. Define synovitis;**
a) A vertebral column congenital disorder
b) Inflammation of a synovial membrane that lines a joint
c) An auto immune disease that attacks the synovial joints
d) A type of arthritis which causes the spine to become rigid

*Answer:* _____

**9. The frontal bone forms;**

a) The cheekbone

b) The lower jaw

c) The upper jaw

d) The forehead

*Answer:* _____

**10. The turbinator bone is located on which part of the face?**

a) Cheek

b) Nose

c) Chin

d) Forehead

*Answer:* _____

**11. What are osteocytes?**

a) Mature periosteum

b) Bone destroying cells

c) Mature osteoclasts

d) Mature osteoblasts

*Answer:* _____

**12. What type of arthritis results in the joints of the spine becoming fused?**

a) Cervical spondylitis

b) Gout

c) Rheumatoid arthritis

d) Ankylosing spondylitis

*Answer:* _____

**13. The back of the skull is made up of which bone?**

a) Occipital

b) Temporal

c) Parietal

d) Lacrimal

*Answer:* _____

**14. Where is the foramen magnus located?**

a) Occipital bone

b) Mandible

c) Parietal bone

d) Frontal

*Answer:* _____

**15. Which part of the body is the cervical spine positioned?**

a) Lower back

b) Ribs

c) Neck

d) Pelvis

*Answer:* _____

**16. How many bones do the lumbar vertebrae contain?**

a) 12

b) 7

c) 4

d) 5

*Answer:* _____

**17. The shoulder blades are called?**

a) Sternum

b) Clavicle

c) Scapulae

d) Ribs

*Answer:* _____

**18. The bone at the top of the arm is called;**

a) Humerus

b) Ulna

c) Radius

d) Carpals

*Answer:* _____

| | |
|---|---|
| **19. The wrist bones are known as;**<br>a) Phalanges<br>b) Metacarpals<br>c) Tarsals<br>d) Carpals<br><br><br><br>*Answer: _____* | **20. How many phalanges are there in each hand?**<br>a) 12<br>b) 14<br>c) 8<br>d) 10<br><br><br>*Answer: _____* |
| **21. A compound fracture describes;**<br>a) The broken part of the bone protruding through the skin<br>b) A partial fracture of a bone occurring in children only<br>c) The broken bone penetrates tissue or organs around it<br>d) A broken bone in 2 or more places<br><br>*Answer: _____* | **22. The anatomical term that describes nearer to the surface is;**<br>a) Superficial<br>b) External<br>c) Internal<br>d) Proximal<br><br><br><br>*Answer: _____* |
| **23. The heel bone is known as;**<br>a) Cuboid bone<br>b) Calcaneus bone<br>c) Navicular bone<br>d) Cuneiform bone<br><br><br><br><br>*Answer: _____* | **24. What are joints?**<br>a) The location at which 2 or more bones meet<br>b) The location at which a tendon meets bone<br>c) The location at which the origin of a muscle meets it's insertion<br>d) The body's muscles<br><br>*Answer: _____* |
| **25. Which of the following is not a cause of postural deformities?**<br>a) Congenital<br>b) Diet<br>c) Bad posture<br>d) Traumatic<br><br>*Answer: _____* | **26. What type of joint is the knee?**<br>a) Gliding<br>b) Saddle<br>c) Hinge<br>d) Pivot<br><br><br><br>*Answer: _____* |

| | |
|---|---|
| **27. Which type of arthritis attacks the synovial lining of joints?**<br>a) Rheumatoid arthritis<br>b) Osteo arthritis<br>c) Degenerative arthritis<br>d) Chronic arthritis<br><br>*Answer:* _____ | **28. What type of bones allow the body to move?**<br>a) Short bones<br>b) Flat bones<br>c) Sesamoid bones<br>d) Long bones<br><br>*Answer:* _____ |
| **29. Which bone helps to form the eye socket?**<br>a) Ethmoid<br>b) Lacrimal<br>c) Sphenoid<br>d) Parietal<br><br>*Answer:* _____ | **30. Which bone joins the foot to the leg?**<br>a) Navicular<br>b) Cuboid<br>c) Cuneiform<br>d) Talus<br><br><br>*Answer:* _____ |
| **31. Which type of joint is the least moveable?**<br>a) Hinge<br>b) Ball & Socket<br>c) Gliding<br>d) Saddle<br><br>*Answer:* _____ | **32. Inflammation of the joints is known as;**<br>a) Gout<br>b) Osteoporosis<br>c) Neuritis<br>d) Arthritis<br><br>*Answer:* _____ |
| **33. Which bone contains the upper teeth?**<br>a) Mandible<br>b) Sphenoid<br>c) Maxilla<br>d) Vomer<br><br>*Answer:* _____ | **34. Which type of vertebrae is not known as true vertebrae?**<br>a) Cervical<br>b) Sacral<br>c) Thoracic<br>d) Lumbar<br><br>*Answer:* _____ |
| **35. How many bones does the coccygeal contain?**<br>a) 4<br>b) 12<br>c) 5<br>d) 7<br><br><br><br><br><br>*Answer:* _____ | **36. What is the structure of slightly moveable joints?**<br>a) Protective pads of fibrocartilage between the bones<br>b) Muscular tissue between the bones<br>c) Fibrous tissue between the ends of the bones<br>d) A pad of fibrocartilage between the ends of bones<br><br>*Answer:* _____ |

**37. The fibula is a type of;**

a) Short bone

b) Irregular bone

c) Flat bone

d) Long bone

Answer: _____

**38. A bone disease;**

a) Osteoporosis

b) Rheumatoid arthritis

c) Fracture

d) Slipped disc

Answer: _____

**39. How many bones does an adult skeleton have?**

a) 240

b) 206

c) 160

d) 200

Answer: _____

**40. Which of the following is a type of sesamoid bone?**

a) Maxilla

b) Patella

c) Humerus

d) Tarsals

Answer: _____

**41. The cheek bone is known as;**

a) Zygomatic

b) Turbinator

c) Frontal

d) Occipital

Answer: _____

**42. Which part of the vertebral column carries the ribs?**

a) Thoracic

b) Lumbar

c) Cervical

d) Coccygeal

Answer: _____

**43. If a body part is lateral, it means;**

a) Away from the midline

b) Above or towards the upper part

c) Near the surface

d) Nearer to the midline of the body

Answer: _____

**44. What is the shaft of a long bone known as?**

a) Periosteum

b) Diaphysis

c) Articular cartilage

d) Epiphysis

Answer: _____

**45. A painful condition caused by the build up of uric acid crystals within the join capsule;**

a) Gout

b) Osteo arthritis

c) Chronic arthritis

d) Poly arthritis

Answer: _____

**46. The shoulder is an example of which type of joint?**

a) Pivot

b) Ball & Socket

c) Saddle

d) Gliding

Answer: _____

| 47. Where is cancellous bone found? | 48. What parts of the body does the axial skeleton support? |
|---|---|
| a) Ends of long bones and in irregular bones | a) Head and neck |
| b) Ends of irregular bones | b) Lower limbs |
| c) Ends of long bones and in short, flat, irregular bones | c) Head, neck, spine, ribs and sternum |
| d) Ends of long bones and in flat bones | d) Shoulder girdle and upper limbs |
| *Answer:* _____ | *Answer:* _____ |
| 49. The kneecap is also known as; | 50. An exaggerated curvature of the upper spine is known as; |
| a) The Femur | a) Lordosis |
| b) The Patella | b) Scoliosis |
| c) The Hyoid | c) Compound Curvature |
| d) The Occipital | d) Kyphosis |
| *Answer:* _____ | *Answer:* _____ |
| 51. The clavicle is more commonly referred to as; | 52. Which of the following is a type of polyarthritis? |
| a) The shoulder blade | a) Gout |
| b) The collar bone | b) Osteo arthritis |
| c) The lower back | c) Acute arthritis |
| d) The breast bone | d) Rheumatoid arthritis |
| *Answer:* _____ | *Answer:* _____ |
| 53. Short bones can be defined as; | 54. How many bones do the cervical vertebrae contain; |
| a) Protective bones with large flat surfaces | a) 12 |
| b) Strong bones where little movement is required | b) 5 |
| c) A bone embedded within a tendon | c) 4 |
| d) Protective pads of fibrocartilage | d) 7 |
| *Answer:* _____ | *Answer:* _____ |
| 55. What type of bone is the hyoid bone? | 56. Which bone divides the nose into the left and right halves? |
| a) Sesamoid bone | a) Vomer |
| b) Flat bone | b) Sphenoid |
| c) Small bone | c) Parietal |
| d) Irregular bone | d) Lacrimal |
| *Answer:* _____ | *Answer:* _____ |

**57. What anatomical term describes towards the midline of the body?**
a) Distal
b) Lateral
c) Proximal
d) Medial

Answer: _____

**58. Superficial describes;**
a) Nearer to the midline of the body
b) The outer surface of the body
c) Nearer to the surface
d) Towards the higher part

Answer: _____

**59. The coccyx is formed by the;**
a) Thoracic
b) Lumbar
c) Sacral
d) Coccygeal

Answer: _____

**60. Which type of joint is the carpometacarpal joint of the thumb?**
a) Hinge
b) Gliding
c) Pivot
d) Saddle

Answer: _____

**61. A disorder of the skeletal system;**
a) Atony
b) Gout
c) Rupture
d) Oedema

Answer: _____

**62. The metacarpals are known as;**
a) Finger bones
b) Toe bones
c) Palm bones
d) Ankle bones

Answer: _____

**63. What cells break down areas of bone tissue?**
a) Osteoblasts
b) Osteocytes
c) Osteoclasts
d) Chondrocytes

Answer: _____

**64. Proximal refers to;**
a) Nearer to the point of origin
b) Further from the point of origin
c) Lower than or towards the lower part
d) Nearer to the surface

Answer: _____

**65. Which one of the following is not found in haversian canals?**
a) Blood vessels
b) Nerves
c) Lymph capillaries
d) Bone marrow

Answer: _____

**66. Which bone is positioned on the inside of each arm towards the thumb?**
a) Radius
b) Humerus
c) Capitate
d) Ulna

Answer: _____

| 67. Sesamoid bones can be defined as; | 68. What type of bone is the ulna? |
|---|---|
| a) The body's levers<br>b) Strong and compact bones<br>c) Bones that are developed within tendons<br>d) Protective bones with broad flat surfaces<br><br>*Answer:* _____ | a) Long bone<br>b) Short bone<br>c) Sesamoid bone<br>d) Irregular bone<br><br><br><br><br>*Answer:* _____ |
| 69. The bone on the sides and base of the cranium is known as; | 70. Fixed vertebrae are; |
| a) Parietal<br>b) Lacrimal<br>c) Occipital<br>d) Temporal<br><br>*Answer:* _____ | a) Cervical<br>b) Sacral and coccygeal<br>c) Lumbar<br>d) Thoracic<br><br><br>*Answer:* _____ |
| 71. Which bone is positioned on the lateral side of each arm towards the little finger? | 72. The zygomatic bone is a type of; |
| a) Humerus<br>b) Ulna<br>c) Carpals<br>d) Radius<br><br>*Answer:* _____ | a) Flat bone<br>b) Sesamoid bone<br>c) Irregular bone<br>d) Short bone<br><br><br>*Answer:* _____ |
| 73. The first 2 cervical vertebrae are known as; | 74. Which one of the following is not a tarsal? |
| a) Fixed vertebrae<br>b) Axial & Appendicular<br>c) Atlas & Axis<br>d) Carpals<br><br>*Answer:* _____ | a) Talus<br>b) Cuboid<br>c) Pisiform<br>d) Calcaneus<br><br>*Answer:* _____ |

| | |
|---|---|
| **75. How many bones do the sacral vertebrae contain;**<br>a) 12<br>b) 5<br>c) 4<br>d) 7<br><br><br>*Answer:* _____ | **76. What is the foramen magnus?**<br>a) An exaggerated inward curvature of the spine<br>b) A large opening in the occipital bone through which the spinal cord passes<br>c) An opening for the passage of the nasolacrimal duct<br>d) A large bone which forms the chin and sides of the face<br><br>*Answer:* _____ |
| **77. Bones with broad , strong, flat surfaces for muscle attachment are known as;**<br>a) Flat bones<br>b) Irregular bones<br>c) Long bones<br>d) Sesamoid bones<br><br>*Answer:* _____ | **78. The mandible is also known as;**<br>a) The forehead<br>b) The upper jaw<br>c) The cheekbone<br>d) The lower jaw<br><br><br><br>*Answer:* _____ |
| **79. The spinal cord is made up of how many vertebrae;**<br>a) 33<br>b) 21<br>c) 23<br>d) 30<br><br><br>*Answer:* _____ | **80. How many metatarsals are there in each foot?**<br>a) 14<br>b) 5<br>c) 10<br>d) 7<br><br><br>*Answer:* _____ |
| **81. Saddle joints allow;**<br>a) Movement in 2 directions<br>b) Flexion, extension, abduction and adduction<br>c) Movement in 1 direction only<br>d) Movement in all directions<br><br>*Answer:* _____ | **82. The lumbar vertebrae is positioned where in the body?**<br>a) Neck<br>b) Pelvis<br>c) Upper back<br>d) Lower back<br><br><br>*Answer:* _____ |

| | |
|---|---|
| **83. What type of joint is the wrist joint?**<br>a) Saddle<br>b) Gliding<br>c) Pivot<br>d) Condyloid<br><br><br>*Answer:* _____ | **84. The process of bone formation is known as?**<br>a) Inversion<br>b) Ossification<br>c) Diffusion<br>d) Mitosis<br><br>*Answer:* _____ |
| **85. What type of arthritis is a chronic inflammatory disease causing severe deformity and impaired mobility?**<br>a) Osteo arthritis<br>b) Ankylosing spondylitis<br>c) Rheumatoid arthritis<br>d) Degenerative arthritis<br><br><br>*Answer:* _____ | **86. What type of bone is the maxilla?**<br>a) Long bone<br>b) Flat bone<br>c) Sesamoid bone<br>d) Irregular bone<br><br><br><br><br><br>*Answer:* _____ |
| **87. Which bone forms the base of the skull?**<br>a) Sphenoid<br>b) Occipital<br>c) Parietal<br>d) Ethmoid<br><br><br>*Answer:* _____ | **88. Where is the hyoid bone positioned?**<br>a) Arm<br>b) Leg<br>c) Nose<br>d) Base of the tongue<br><br><br><br>*Answer:* _____ |
| **89. Synovial joints are known as;**<br>a) Slightly moveable joints<br>b) Fibrous joints<br>c) Fixed joints<br>d) Freely moveable joints<br><br><br>*Answer:* _____ | **90. The ankle is an example of which type of joint?**<br>a) Pivot<br>b) Hinge<br>c) Gliding<br>d) Saddle<br><br><br>*Answer:* _____ |
| **91. Which one of the following is an effect of osteoarthritis?**<br>a) Chronic destruction of joints<br>b) Severe deformity<br>c) Cartilage of joints break down with eventual loss<br>d) Brittleness of bones<br><br>*Answer:* _____ | **92. Which bone contains the lower teeth?**<br>a) Parietal<br>b) Vomer<br>c) Mandible<br>d) Hyoid<br><br><br><br><br>*Answer:* _____ |

| | |
|---|---|
| **93. How many bones do the thoracic vertebrae have?**<br>a) 5<br>b) 12<br>c) 7<br>d) 4<br><br>*Answer:* _____ | **94. Which bone is positioned on the medial lower leg?**<br>a) Radius<br>b) Patella<br>c) Fibula<br>d) Talus<br><br>*Answer:* _____ |
| **95. The anatomical term, palmar, refers to;**<br>a) The palm of the hand<br>b) The inner surface of the body<br>c) The sole of the foot<br>d) Lying face up<br><br><br>*Answer:* _____ | **96. What type of fracture describes a broken bone with minimal damage to the surrounding tissue?**<br>a) Simple<br>b) Greenstick<br>c) Impacted<br>d) Compound<br><br>*Answer:* _____ |
| **97. What type of bone is the vomer?**<br>a) Short<br>b) Long<br>c) Sesamoid<br>d) Flat<br><br><br><br><br><br><br><br>*Answer:* _____ | **98. Where is compact bone found?**<br>a) On the outer layer of all bones and in the shaft of long bones<br>b) On the ends of long bones and flat bones<br>c) On the inside of most bones and in the shaft of long bones<br>d) On the outside of flat and irregular bones and in the shaft of long bones<br><br>*Answer:* _____ |
| **99. What part of the skull does the parietal bone form?**<br>a) Back of the skull<br>b) Front of the skull<br>c) Sides of the skull<br>d) Top and sides of the skull<br><br>*Answer:* _____ | **100. The finger bones are called;**<br>a) The phalanges<br>b) The carpals<br>c) The metatarsals<br>d) The metacarpals<br><br><br>*Answer:* _____ |

**101. What anatomical direction describes being towards the back?**

a) Dorsal

b) Ventral

c) Superior

d) Proximal

Answer: _____

**102. Define epiphysis;**

a) The shaft of a long bone

b) The hyaline cartilage within bone

c) One or 2 rounded endings of a long bone

d) The membrane surrounding the bone

Answer: _____

**103. Which one of the following is not a type of postural deformity?**

a) Scoliosis

b) Kyphosis

c) Lordosis

d) Osteoporosis

Answer: _____

**104. Degenerative arthritis is also known as;**

a) Acute arthritis

b) Osteoarthritis

c) Rheumatoid arthritis

d) Chronic arthritis

Answer: _____

**105. What type of cells are bones made of?**

a) Osteoblasts

b) Chemoreceptors

c) Erythrocytes

d) Monocytes

Answer: _____

**106. Which bone is found on the roof of the mouth?**

a) Mandible

b) Palatine

c) Vomer

d) Maxilla

Answer: _____

**107. Which of the following is not part of the innominate bone?**

a) Ilium

b) Sacrum

c) Ischium

d) Pubis

Answer: _____

**108. The ankle/heel bones are known as;**

a) Tarsals

b) Metacarpals

c) Carpals

d) Metatarsals

Answer: _____

**109. What anatomical direction refers to lower than or towards the lower part?**

a) Medial

b) Caudal

c) Deep

d) Anterior

Answer: _____

**110. The anatomical terms that describes lying face up is;**

a) Supine

b) Superficial

c) Anterior

d) Lateral

Answer: _____

| | |
|---|---|
| **111. Which joint allows rotation?**<br>a) Gliding<br>b) Ball & Socket<br>c) Pivot<br>d) Saddle<br><br><br>*Answer:* _____ | **112. Which one of the following is a tarsal bone?**<br>a) Capitate<br>b) Triquetral<br>c) Trapezoid<br>d) Navicular<br><br>*Answer:* _____ |
| **113. Which one of the following is a type of flat bone?**<br>a) Patella<br>b) Mandible<br>c) Nasal<br>d) Temporal<br><br>*Answer:* _____ | **114. What type of bone resembles honeycomb?**<br>a) Cancellous bone<br>b) Sesamoid bone<br>c) Compact bone<br>d) Bone marrow<br><br>*Answer:* _____ |
| **115. Which bone is the only moveable bone on the face?**<br>a) Mandible<br>b) Maxilla<br>c) Occipital<br>d) Frontal<br><br>*Answer:* _____ | **116. What bones fuse to form the sacrum?**<br>a) Sacral vertebrae<br>b) Thoracic vertebrae<br>c) Cervical vertebrae<br>d) Coccygeal<br><br>*Answer:* _____ |
| **117. Fibrous joints;**<br>a) Are freely moveable<br>b) Are slightly moveable<br>c) Have no movement<br>d) Move in one direction<br><br><br>*Answer:* _____ | **118. The elbow is an example of which type of joint?**<br>a) Hinge<br>b) Saddle<br>c) Fixed<br>d) Ball & Socket<br><br><br>*Answer:* _____ |
| **119. Which bone provides attachment for the tongue?**<br>a) Sphenoid<br>b) Ethmoid<br>c) Hyoid<br>d) Mandible<br><br>*Answer:* _____ | **120. Which one of the following bones does not form the pelvis?**<br>a) Innominate bones<br>b) Coccyx<br>c) Sacrum<br>d) Femur<br><br>*Answer:* _____ |

| | |
|---|---|
| **121. The anatomical direction ventral describes;**<br>a) Away from the midline<br>b) In front of<br>c) Behind<br>d) Further from the surface<br><br>*Answer:* _____ | **122. Where can osteoblasts be found?**<br>a) The outer layer of the periosteum<br>b) The shaft of the bone<br>c) The inner layer of the periosteum<br>d) Compact bone<br><br>*Answer:* _____ |
| **123. Which type of synovial joint is the most moveable?**<br>a) Ball & Socket<br>b) Hinge<br>c) Gliding<br>d) Pivot<br><br>*Answer:* _____ | **124. An increased inward curvature of the spine is known as;**<br>a) Lordosis<br>b) Impacted curvature<br>c) Kyphosis<br>d) Scoliosis<br><br>*Answer:* _____ |
| **125. The breast bone is also known as;**<br>a) The clavicle<br>b) The scapulae<br>c) The sternum<br>d) The pelvic girdle<br><br>*Answer:* _____ | **126. Joints which allow movement in one plane only are called?**<br>a) Hinge joints<br>b) Saddle joints<br>c) Pivot joints<br>d) Ball & socket joints<br><br>*Answer:* _____ |
| **127. How many tarsals are there in each ankle?**<br>a) 14<br>b) 7<br>c) 5<br>d) 10<br><br>*Answer:* _____ | **128. Where is the lacrimal bone positioned?**<br>a) Forehead<br>b) In the nasal cavity<br>c) Eye socket<br>d) Cheek<br><br>*Answer:* _____ |
| **129. Where is bone marrow found?**<br>a) Compact bone<br>b) Haversian canals<br>c) Cancellous bone<br>d) Sesamoid bones<br><br>*Answer:* _____ | **130. The broad, upper, flat part of the sternum is called;**<br>a) Manubrium<br>b) Phalanges<br>c) Clavicle<br>d) Innominate bone<br><br>*Answer:* _____ |

**131. What type of fracture occurs when a bone is broken and is driven into another bone?**
a) Greenstick
b) Comminuted
c) Impacted
d) Simple

*Answer:* _____

**132. The anatomical term that describes further from the point of origin is;**
a) Plantar
b) Proximal
c) Distal
d) Dorsal

*Answer:* _____

**133. How many carpals are there in each wrist?**
a) 5
b) 14
c) 6
d) 8

*Answer:* _____

**134. Cartilaginous joints are also known as;**
a) Slightly moveable joints
b) Pivot joints
c) Freely moveable joints
d) Fixed joints

*Answer:* _____

**135. Scoliosis causes;**
a) An increased inward curvature of the lower spine
b) A curvature of the spine from side to side
c) An increased outward curvature of the upper spine
d) Exaggerated rounded shoulders

*Answer:* _____

**136. Tarsals fall under which category of bone;**
a) Long bones
b) Irregular bones
c) Short bones
d) Sesamoid bones

*Answer:* _____

**137. The anatomical term, plantar, refers to;**
a) The palm of the hand
b) The sole of the foot
c) Lying face down
d) Towards the midline of the body

*Answer:* _____

**138. Which one of the following is a function of periosteum?**
a) To provide attachment for tendons, ligaments and muscles
b) To produce bone forming cells
c) To protect bones against disease and infection
d) To manufacture red bone marrow

*Answer:* _____

**139. Which one of the following is a type of irregular bone?**

a) Sphenoid
b) Lacrimal
c) Metacarpals
d) Scapula

Answer: _____

**140. What bone forms the nasolacrimal ducts?**

a) Frontal
b) Lacrimal
c) Ethmoid
d) Temporal

Answer: _____

**141. How many metacarpals are there in each hand?**

a) 5
b) 8
c) 12
d) 4

Answer: _____

**142. Which one of the following is a wrist bone?**

a) Calcaneus
b) Sphenoid
c) Hamate
d) Ethmoid

Answer: _____

**143. What is the thigh bone called?**

a) Femur
b) Tibia
c) Fibula
d) Tarsal

Answer: _____

**144. Fixed joints are also known as;**

a) Cartilaginous
b) Fibrous
c) Synovial
d) Hinge

Answer: _____

**145. Which of the following is an example of a long bone?**

a) Carpals
b) Clavicle
c) Zygomatic
d) Maxilla

Answer: _____

**146. Which one of the following is not a wrist bone?**

a) Trapezium
b) Capitate
c) Lunate
d) Medial

Answer: _____

**147. What are cartilage forming cells called?**

a) Chondrocytes
b) Osteoclasts
c) Erythrocytes
d) Thrombocytes

Answer: _____

**148. What type of joint allows movement in 2 directions?**

a) Condyloid
b) Pivot
c) Fibrous
d) Hinge

Answer: _____

**149. The anatomical term that describes being further from the surface is;**
a) Medial
b) Superficial
c) Proximal
d) Deep

*Answer:* _____

# The Skeletal System - Crossword 1

**Across**

4. Ankle bone (9)
8. Upper jaw bone (7)
10. What do haversian canals contain? (6)
12. Kneecap (7)
14. What type of bone is the humerus? (4)
15. A sideways curvature of the vertebral column (9)
17. Wrist bone (8)

**Down**

1. Shoulder blade (7)
2. What type of bone is the sternum? (4)
3. What part of the body is the fibula found? (3)
5. Freely moveable joints (9)
6. The sacral and coccygeal vertebrae (5)
7. A term for ankle bones (7)
9. Where is the calcaneus bone found? (4)
11. Which one of these bones forms the pelvis? (6)
13. Lower leg bone (5)
16. Cube shaped, strong bones (5)

# The Skeletal System - Crossword 2

## Across

1. Bone that joins the foot to the leg (5)
4. A condition caused by brittle bones (12)
7. Lower back (6)
10. Thigh bone (5)
13. Only moveable bone of the skull (8)
15. Part of the skeleton that supports head, neck and trunk (5)
16. Bone of lower arm (4)
17. Bones that allow movement (4)

## Down

2. Breast bone (7)
3. Where is the ulna found? (3)
5. Function of skeleton (7)
6. What type of bone is found on the ends of long bones? (10)
8. Bones found within tendons (8)
9. Bone of forehead (7)
11. Joints where no movement is possible (5)
12. Bones which help to protect vital organs (4)
14. A joint which moves in one direction only (5)

## The Skeletal System - Crossword 3

### Across

4. Bone that forms the sides of the skull under the parietal bones (8)
6. Part of the skeleton that supports the limbs (12)
7. A long bone (4)
9. An increased curvature of the lumbar spine (8)
10. Bone at the base of the tongue (5)
11. What is the top part of the sternum called? (9)
12. Location of the metatarsals (4)
13. Part of the spine that carries the ribs (8)

### Down

1. Function of skeleton (10)
2. Innominate bones help form this (6)
3. Which joint allows movement in most directions? (13)
5. What part of the body is the radius bone found? (3)
8. Bone tissue found on the outer layer of most bones (7)

# The Skeletal System - Crossword 4

**Across**

6. What part of the skeleton supports the ribs? (5)

7. Collar bone (8)

10. Where is the humerus found? (3)

12. What part of the body is the cervical spine positioned? (4)

13. A postural deformity (8)

16. What type of cells make up bone tissue? (11)

18. A sesamoid bone (7)

19. Function of the skeleton (8)

20. Vertebrae of the lower back (6)

**Down**

1. A bone found at the base of the tongue in the neck (5)
2. Where is the frontal bone positioned? (8)
3. Protective bones with broad surfaces (4)
4. What type of joint is the shoulder joint? (13)
5. Heel bone (9)
8. Slightly moveable joints (13)
9. What type of bones are the tarsals? (5)
11. Bone which forms the back of the skull? (9)
14. Finger bones (9)
15. A type of arthritis which affects the big toe? (4)
17. What type of bone is the femur? (4)

# The Skeletal System - Crossword 5

## Across

1. A disease of the joints (9)
3. Function of the skeleton (7)
6. Which bone holds the upper teeth? (7)
7. What category of bone enables the body to move? (4)
9. Where is the zygomatic bone positioned? (5)
12. A disease that weakens the bones (12)
14. What bones form the bridge of the nose? (5)
16. What type of bone tissue is found at the ends of long bones? (10)
17. Upper arm bone (7)
18. Ilium, ischium and pubis (15)
19. The thigh bone (5)
20. What bone forms the ankle joint? (5)

**Down**

2. Which part of the vertebral column carries the ribs? (8)
4. A wrist bone (10)
5. Freely moveable joints (8)
8. Hand bones (11)
10. What allows the bone to move in different directions? (6)
11. What type of joint is the elbow joint? (5)
13. An increased curvature of the spine to the left or right (9)
15. What flat bone is positioned in the middle of the chest? (7)

# The Skeletal System – Crossword 6

**Across**

1. What type of bone is the patella? (8)
4. Where can you find red bone marrow? (14)
5. Lower arm bone (6)
6. What bone forms the eye socket and nasal cavities? (7)
7. Vertebrae fused together to form the coccyx (9)
14. Wrist bone (6)
17. A bone in the cranium (8)
18. Lower leg bone (6)
19. Vertebrae that can move (4)
20. What part of the skeleton comprises the shoulder girdle? (12)

**Down**

2. What bone of the skull holds the lower teeth? (8)
3. A type of synovial joint (6)
8. What type of bone tissue contains haversian canals? (7)
9. An exaggerated curvature of the thoracic spine (8)
10. Fixed joints (7)
11. A type of arthritis (10)
12. A thin layer of connective tissue covering bones (10)
13. Ankle bone (6)
15. Bone of the shoulder girdle (7)
16. What part of the vertebrae forms the sacrum? (6)

## Multiple Choice Answers – The Skeletal System

| # | Ans | # | Ans | # | Ans | # | Ans | # | Ans | # | Ans |
|---|---|---|---|---|---|---|---|---|---|---|---|
| 1 | A | 26 | C | 51 | B | 76 | B | 101 | A | 126 | A |
| 2 | D | 27 | A | 52 | D | 77 | A | 102 | C | 127 | B |
| 3 | B | 28 | D | 53 | B | 78 | D | 103 | D | 128 | C |
| 4 | C | 29 | A | 54 | D | 79 | A | 104 | B | 129 | C |
| 5 | B | 30 | D | 55 | A | 80 | B | 105 | A | 130 | A |
| 6 | B | 31 | C | 56 | A | 81 | B | 106 | B | 131 | C |
| 7 | D | 32 | D | 57 | D | 82 | D | 107 | B | 132 | C |
| 8 | B | 33 | C | 58 | C | 83 | D | 108 | A | 133 | D |
| 9 | D | 34 | B | 59 | D | 84 | B | 109 | B | 134 | A |
| 10 | B | 35 | A | 60 | D | 85 | B | 110 | A | 135 | B |
| 11 | D | 36 | A | 61 | B | 86 | D | 111 | C | 136 | C |
| 12 | D | 37 | D | 62 | C | 87 | A | 112 | D | 137 | B |
| 13 | A | 38 | A | 63 | C | 88 | D | 113 | C | 138 | A |
| 14 | A | 39 | B | 64 | A | 89 | D | 114 | C | 139 | A |
| 15 | C | 40 | B | 65 | D | 90 | B | 115 | A | 140 | B |
| 16 | D | 41 | A | 66 | A | 91 | C | 116 | A | 141 | A |
| 17 | C | 42 | A | 67 | C | 92 | C | 117 | C | 142 | C |
| 18 | A | 43 | A | 68 | A | 93 | B | 118 | A | 143 | A |
| 19 | D | 44 | B | 69 | D | 94 | C | 119 | C | 144 | B |
| 20 | B | 45 | A | 70 | B | 95 | A | 120 | D | 145 | B |
| 21 | A | 46 | B | 71 | B | 96 | A | 121 | B | 146 | D |
| 22 | B | 47 | C | 72 | C | 97 | D | 122 | C | 147 | A |
| 23 | B | 48 | C | 73 | C | 98 | A | 123 | A | 148 | A |
| 24 | A | 49 | B | 74 | C | 99 | D | 124 | A | 149 | D |
| 25 | B | 50 | D | 75 | B | 100 | A | 125 | C | | |

## Crossword Answers – The Skeletal System

### Crossword 1

**Across**
4. Calcaneus
8. Maxilla
10. Nerves
12. Patella
14. Long
15. Scoliosis
17. Pisiform

**Down**
1. Scapula
2. Flat
3. Leg
5. Snynovial
6. False
7. Tarsals
9. Heel
11. Sacrum
13. Tibia
16. Short

### Crossword 2

**Across**
1. Talus
4. Osteoporosis
7. Lumbar
10. Femur
13. Mandible
15. Axial
16. Ulna
17. Long

**Down**
2. Sternum
3. Arm
5. Support
6. Cancellous
8. Sesamoid
9. Frontal
11. Fixed
12. Flat
14. Hinge

### Crossword 3

**Across**
4. Temporal
6. Appendicular
7. Ulna
9. Lordosis
10. Hyoid
11. Manubrium
12. Feet
13. Thoracic

**Down**
1. Protection
2. Pelvis
3. Ball and Socket
5. Arm
8. Compact

### Crossword 4

**Across**
6. Axial
7. Clavicle
10. Arm
12. Neck
13. Lordosis
16. Osteoblasts
18. Patella
19. Movement
20. Lumbar

**Down**
1. Hyoid
2. Forehead
3. Flat
4. Ball and Socket
5. Calcaneus
8. Cartilaginous
9. Short
11. Occipital
14. Phalanges
15. Gout
17. Long

### Crossword 5

**Across**
1. Arthritis
3. Support
6. Maxilla
7. Long
9. Cheek
12. Osteoporosis
14. Nasal
16. Cancellous

**Down**
2. Thoracic
4. Triquetral
5. Synovial
8. Metacarpals
10. Joints
11. Hinge
13. Scoliosis
15. Sternum
17. Humerus
18. Innominate Bones
19. Femur
20. Talus

### Crossword 6

**Across**
1. Sesamoid
4. Cancellous Bone
5. Radius
6. Ethmoid
7. Coccygeal
14. Lunate
17. Temporal
18. Fibula
19. True
20. Appendicular

**Down**
2. Mandible
3. Saddle
8. Compact
9. Kyphosis
10. Fibrous
11. Rheumatoid
12. Periosteum
13. Cuboid
15. Scapula
16. Sacral

# Chapter 4 | The Muscular System

## Multiple Choice Questions

| | |
|---|---|
| **1. Turning the hand to face upwards is known as;**<br>a) Plantarflexion<br>b) Pronation<br>c) Supination<br>d) Eversion<br><br>*Answer:* _____ | **2. Which muscle helps to bend the neck laterally?**<br>a) Mentalis<br>b) Ilio psoas<br>c) Levator scapulae<br>d) Masseter<br><br>*Answer:* _____ |
| **3. What is the position of the flexor carpi radialis?**<br>a) Posterior forearm<br>b) Palm of hand<br>c) Elbow<br>d) Top of humerus<br><br>*Answer:* _____ | **4. What is the structure of muscle tissue?**<br>a) Muscle tissue has spindle shaped cells with a nucleus<br>b) Muscle tissue is bound together in bundles and enclosed in a sheath<br>c) Muscle tissue has striated fibres with only 1 nucleus<br>d) Muscle tissue is made up of several nuclei and is enclosed by a sheath<br><br>*Answer:* _____ |
| **5. The agonist muscle is;**<br>a) The relaxing muscle<br>b) The fixed end of the muscle<br>c) The contracting muscle<br>d) The thickest part of the muscle<br><br>*Answer:* _____ | **6. Which of the following is not an action of the pectoralis major?**<br>a) Draws arm backwards<br>b) Draws arm forwards<br>c) Medially rotates arm<br>d) Adducts humerus<br><br>*Answer:* _____ |
| **7. Which muscle flexes the hip?**<br>a) Biceps femoris<br>b) Vastus lateralis<br>c) Gastrocnemius<br>d) Rectus femoris<br><br>*Answer:* _____ | **8. The muscular system relies on the skeletal system for which of the following?**<br>a) Production of heat<br>b) Production of nerve impulses<br>c) Movement<br>d) Storage of glycogen<br><br>*Answer:* _____ |

**9. Which muscle raises the eyebrows?**

a) Frontalis

b) Risorius

c) Procerus nasi

d) Occipitofrontalis

Answer: _____

**10. Where are the rhomboids positioned?**

a) Waist

b) Between scapula and spine

c) Top of scapula

d) Scapula

Answer: _____

**11. What muscle lowers the mandible and opens the mouth?**

a) Lateral pterygoid

b) Medial pterygoid

c) Orbicularis oculi

d) Masseter

Answer: _____

**12. What is the action of the sternocleidomastoid?**

a) Elevates scapula

b) Draws scapula backwards

c) Bends neck laterally

d) Flexes head

Answer: _____

**13. Which muscle laterally rotates humerus?**

a) Supraspinatus

b) Teres major

c) Trapezius

d) Infraspinatus

Answer: _____

**14. Voluntary muscle is also known as;**

a) Smooth muscle

b) Cardiac muscle

c) Unstriated muscle

d) Skeletal muscle

Answer: _____

**15. What is the action of the frontalis?**

a) Raises lower jaw

b) Draws scalp forwards

c) Shows a disgusted expression

d) Moves scalp backwards

Answer: _____

**16. Where is the ilio psoas positioned?**

a) Deep to the gluteus minimus

b) Underneath the gluteus maximus

c) Across the hip joint

d) Underneath the gluteus medius

Answer: _____

**17. What is the action of the biceps?**

a) Flexes wrist joint

b) Pronates forearm

c) Supinates forearm

d) Flexes fingers

Answer: _____

**18. What muscle crosses the elbow joint?**

a) Flexor carpi ulnaris

b) Brachialis

c) Extensor carpi radialis

d) Triceps

Answer: _____

| | |
|---|---|
| **19. A sudden twist in ligaments around a joint is known as?**<br>a) Sprain<br>b) Strain<br>c) Rupture<br>d) Spasm<br><br>*Answer:* _____ | **20. What is the strongest muscle in the body?**<br>a) Deltoids<br>b) Latissimus dorsi<br>c) Hamstrings<br>d) Gluteus maximus<br><br>*Answer:* _____ |
| **21. What is the structure of a tendon?**<br>a) White fibrous elastic tissue<br>b) White fibrous adipose tissue<br>c) White fibrous elastic cords<br>d) White fibrous inelastic cords<br><br>*Answer:* _____ | **22. Where is the risorius positioned?**<br>a) Around the eye<br>b) From the masseter to the corner of the mouth<br>c) Behind the cheek bone<br>d) Upper eyelid<br><br>*Answer:* _____ |
| **23. Where is the rectus abdominus positioned?**<br>a) Side of thorax<br>b) Deep to the transverse abdominus<br>c) Waist<br>d) Abdominal wall<br><br>*Answer:* _____ | **24. Which muscle flexes the wrist?**<br>a) Flexor carpi digitorum<br>b) Flexor digitorum superficialis<br>c) Brachioradialis<br>d) Flexor carpi radialis<br><br>*Answer:* _____ |
| **25. What muscle extends the hip?**<br>a) Adductor magnus<br>b) Vastus intermedius<br>c) Soleus<br>d) Biceps femoris<br><br><br><br>*Answer:* _____ | **26. What is the composition of muscle?**<br>a) 75% water, 20% protein, 5% mineral salts, fats and glycogen<br>b) 75% water, 15% protein, 10% mineral salts, fats and glucose<br>c) 75% water, 20% protein, 5% mineral salts, fats and maltase<br>d) 75% water and 25% protein<br><br>*Answer:* _____ |
| **27. Where is superficial fascia found?**<br>a) Surrounding the muscle<br>b) Top layer of the skin<br>c) Under the skin<br>d) Surrounding the tendon<br><br>*Answer:* _____ | **28. What is the action of the trapezius?**<br>a) Flexes head<br>b) Draws arm forward<br>c) Adducts scapula<br>d) Bend neck laterally<br><br>*Answer:* _____ |

**29. What is the position of the biceps?**
a) Back of the upper arm
b) Elbow
c) Posterior forearm
d) Front of the upper arm

Answer: _____

**30. What muscle is positioned on the front of the lower leg?**
a) Soleus
b) Gastrocnemius
c) Flexor digitorum longus
d) Tibialis anterior

Answer: _____

**31. Which one of the following is a disorder of the muscular system?**
a) Arthritis
b) Spasticity
c) Bursitis
d) Lordosis

Answer: _____

**32. Which one of the following muscles is not part of the quadriceps?**
a) Vastus lateralis
b) Rectus femoris
c) Biceps femoris
d) Vastus medialis

Answer: _____

**33. Where is the coracobrachialis positioned?**
a) Lower arm
b) Elbow
c) Humerus
d) Anterior forearm

Answer: _____

**34. What is the deepest muscle of the abdomen?**
a) Transverse abdominis
b) Rectus abdominis
c) Internal oblique
d) External oblique

Answer: _____

**35. What muscle elevates the mandible?**
a) Sternocleidomastoid
b) Medial pterygoid
c) Lateral pterygoid
d) Buccinator

Answer: _____

**36. The origin of a muscle is known as;**
a) The main body of the muscle
b) The attachment of the muscle to tendons
c) The end of the muscle that is stationary
d) The moving end of the muscle

Answer: _____

**37. Which muscle covers the frontal bone?**
a) Mentalis
b) Occipitalis
c) Nasalis
d) Frontalis

Answer: _____

**38. Where is the brachialis positioned?**
a) Posterior upper arm
b) Anterior upper arm
c) Posterior forearm
d) Anterior forearm

Answer: _____

**39. How does the muscular system rely on the respiratory system?**
a) Muscles receive oxygen from the respiratory system for energy
b) Muscles receive glucose from the respiratory system for energy
c) Muscles receive nerve impulses from the respiratory system for movement
d) Muscles receive glycogen from the respiratory system for heat production

*Answer:* _____

**40. Which muscle extends the wrist?**
a) Extensor carpi digitorum
b) Pronator teres
c) Extensor carpi ulnaris
d) Anconeus

*Answer:* _____

**41. Which muscle is positioned on the inner thigh?**
a) Biceps femoris
b) Vastus lateralis
c) Gracilis
d) Soleus

*Answer:* _____

**42. Which one of the following is not a function of muscle?**
a) Produce movement
b) Maintain posture
c) Production of heat
d) Protects organs

*Answer:* _____

**43. Lactic acid is caused by;**
a) Inadequate blood supply in the muscle
b) Temperature of the muscle
c) Insufficient oxygen in the muscle
d) Over stimulation of a nerve impulse in the muscle

*Answer:* _____

**44. Pronation describes;**
a) Flexion of the foot downwards
b) Turning the palm of the hand to face downwards
c) Moving the arm towards the midline
d) Turning the foot towards the centre

*Answer:* _____

**45. What muscle pulls the lower lip down?**
a) Depressor labii inferioris
b) Depressor anguli oris
c) Orbicularis oculi
d) Buccinator

*Answer:* _____

**46. What muscle draws the scapula forward?**
a) Serratus anterior
b) Middle deltoid
c) Internal oblique
d) Posterior deltoid

*Answer:* _____

| | |
|---|---|
| **47. What is the position of the pronator teres?**<br>a) Anterior forearm<br>b) Posterior forearm<br>c) Elbow<br>d) Wrist<br><br>*Answer:* _____ | **48. What is the action of the vastus medialis?**<br>a) Flexes knee<br>b) Extends knee<br>c) Flexes hip<br>d) Extends hip<br><br>*Answer:* _____ |
| **49. Which of the following is an involuntary action?**<br>a) Lifting an arm<br>b) Heartbeat<br>c) Rotation of the head<br>d) Moving fingers<br><br>*Answer:* _____ | **50. Inflammation of a muscle is known as;**<br>a) Myositis<br>b) Fibrositis<br>c) Spasticity<br>d) Rupture<br><br>*Answer:* _____ |
| **51. Which muscle flexes the forearm at the elbow?**<br>a) Brachioradialis<br>b) Pronator teres<br>c) Anconeus<br>d) Extensor carpi radialis<br><br>*Answer:* _____ | **52. What is the structure of voluntary muscle?**<br>a) Bundles of nerve cells surrounded by unmyelinated sheath<br>b) Spindle shaped cells with no nucleus<br>c) Bundles of muscle fibres surrounded by a sheath<br>d) Striated fibres with a membrane and nucleus<br><br>*Answer:* _____ |
| **53. Which one of the following is not a function of superficial fascia?**<br>a) Helps retain body warmth<br>b) Connects skin with deep fascia<br>c) Allows movement of the skin<br>d) Connects muscles with deep fascia<br><br>*Answer:* _____ | **54. What muscle helps with chewing?**<br>a) Buccinator<br>b) Masseter<br>c) Orbicularis oculi<br>d) Depressor anguli oris<br><br><br><br>*Answer:* _____ |
| **55. Which muscle extends the hip?**<br>a) Ilio psoas<br>b) Gluteus minimus<br>c) Gluteus medius<br>d) Gluteus maximus<br><br><br>*Answer:* _____ | **56. What is the position of the brachioradialis?**<br>a) Anterior humerus<br>b) Anterior elbow<br>c) Posterior forearm<br>d) Anterior forearm<br><br><br>*Answer:* _____ |

**57. What is the action of the rectus femoris?**

a) Flex knee

b) Extend hip

c) Extend knee

d) Extends foot

Answer: _____

**58. What muscle supports the arches of the feet?**

a) Sartorius

b) Peroneus longus

c) Tibialis anterior

d) Soleus

Answer: _____

**59. What muscle flexes the knee?**

a) Semitendinosus

b) Peroneus Longus

c) Soleus

d) Tibialis anterior

Answer: _____

**60. Which one of the following is not a cause of a strain?**

a) Over use

b) Over exertion

c) Over stretching

d) Over heating

Answer: _____

**61. What muscle in the body has the largest surface area?**

a) Gluteus maximus

b) Latissimus dorsi

c) Trapezius

d) Rhomboids

Answer: _____

**62. Isometric contraction occurs;**

a) When the tension in a muscle increases but it's length is not altered

b) When the muscle stretches and moves

c) When the tension in the muscle remains the same but it's length is increased

d) When the muscle contracts

Answer: _____

**63. What is a muscle's fuel?**

a) Lactic acid

b) Glucose

c) Oxyhaemoglobin

d) Blood

Answer: _____

**64. What muscle draws the scalp backwards?**

a) Frontalis

b) Buccinator

c) Occipitalis

d) Levator labii superioris

Answer: _____

**65. Which muscle forms the wall of the cheek?**

a) Mandible

b) Maxilla

c) Risorius

d) Buccinator

Answer: _____

**66. Where is the transverse abdominis positioned?**

a) Waist

b) Beneath the internal obliques

c) Side of thorax

d) Pelvic floor

Answer: _____

| | |
|---|---|
| **67. What is the action of the peroneus longus?**<br>a) Everts foot<br>b) Plantarflexes foot<br>c) Everts and plantarflexes foot<br>d) Extends toes<br><br>*Answer:* _____ | **68. Which muscle is not part of the hamstrings group?**<br>a) Vastus lateralis<br>b) Semitendinosus<br>c) Biceps femoris<br>d) Semimembranosus<br><br>*Answer:* _____ |
| **69. Atrophy can be described as;**<br>a) Inflammation of a muscle<br>b) A build up of lactic acid on a muscle<br>c) Wasting away of muscle tissue<br>d) Injury to a joint<br><br>*Answer:* _____ | **70. Smooth muscle is also known as;**<br>a) Skeletal muscle<br>b) Involuntary muscle<br>c) Voluntary muscle<br>d) Cardiac muscle<br><br>*Answer:* _____ |
| **71. What type of muscle contraction occurs when it's length changes and the tension stays the same?**<br>a) Isometric contraction<br>b) Antagonist<br>c) Isotonic contraction<br>d) Muscle attachment<br><br>*Answer:* _____ | **72. Which one of the following is not an action of the teres major?**<br>a) Rotates scapula<br>b) Adducts humerus<br>c) Medially rotates humerus<br>d) Extends shoulder joint<br><br><br><br>*Answer:* _____ |
| **73. Which muscle adducts the humerus?**<br>a) Infraspinatus<br>b) Pronator teres<br>c) Brachioradialis<br>d) Teres major<br><br>*Answer:* _____ | **74. What is the action of the brachialis?**<br>a) Extend elbow joint<br>b) Extends wrist<br>c) Flexes elbow joint<br>d) Flexes wrist<br><br>*Answer:* _____ |
| **75. Which muscle is positioned on the front of the thigh?**<br>a) Gracilis<br>b) Rectus femoris<br>c) Biceps femoris<br>d) Adductor magnus<br><br>*Answer:* _____ | **76. What is the action of the gastrocnemius?**<br>a) Flexes toes<br>b) Extends toes<br>c) Extends foot<br>d) Plantarflexes foot<br><br>*Answer:* _____ |

**77. Which of the following is not a cause of a cramp?**

a) Vigorous exercise

b) Heat

c) Dehydration

d) Lack of calcium in the muscle

*Answer:* _____

**78. Which one of the following muscle is not part of the adductor group?**

a) Adductor brevis

b) Adductor medialis

c) Adductor longus

d) Adductor magnus

*Answer:* _____

**79. Which muscle flexes the elbow?**

a) Triceps

b) Biceps

c) Flexor carpi ulnaris

d) Flexor carpi radialis

*Answer:* _____

**80. What muscle laterally rotates the femur?**

a) Adductor magnus

b) Vastus lateralis

c) Peroneus longus

d) Ilio psoas

*Answer:* _____

**81. What is the structure of involuntary muscle?**

a) Spindle shaped muscle cells with one nucleus

b) Striated fibres with a membrane

c) Muscle fibres held together by elastic tissue

d) Spindle shaped muscle cells with no nucleus

*Answer:* _____

**82. What is the function of a tendon?**

a) It attaches muscle to bone

b) It attaches bone to ligaments

c) It attaches the origin of a muscle to its insertion point

d) It attaches muscle to ligaments

*Answer:* _____

**83. What is the action of the masseter?**

a) Opens upper eyelid

b) Lifts upper lip

c) Raises mandible

d) Closes eyelid

*Answer:* _____

**84. Which muscle elevates the mandible?**

a) Sternocleidomastoid

b) Medial pterygoid

c) Lateral pterygoid

d) Temporalis

*Answer:* _____

**85. Which muscle rotates the head to the opposite side?**

a) Levator scapulae

b) Sternocleidomastoid

c) Trapezius

d) Masseter

*Answer:* _____

**86. Which muscle lies beneath the biceps?**

a) Brachialis

b) Brachioradialis

c) Anconeus

d) Teres minor

*Answer:* _____

**87. Where is the tendon of achilles positioned?**

a) Lower leg
b) Thigh
c) Knee
d) Elbow

*Answer:* _____

**88. Fibromyalgia affects what part of the body?**

a) Lower back
b) Hands
c) Back, neck and shoulders
d) Face

*Answer:* _____

**89. What is the action of the temporalis?**

a) Opens mouth
b) Lowers the lower jaw
c) Flexes head
d) Raises the lower jaw

*Answer:* _____

**90. What is the position of the occipitalis?**

a) At the back of the head
b) At the side of the head
c) Sides of the nose
d) At the top of the head

*Answer:* _____

**91. What is the structure of cardiac muscle?**

a) Spindle shaped muscle cells with no nucleus
b) Cylindrical cells with no nucleus and a membrane
c) Non striated fibres with a nucleus
d) Striated fibres

*Answer:* _____

**92. What muscle does not flex the hip?**

a) Vastus lateralis
b) Sartorius
c) Rectus femoris
d) Ilio psoas

*Answer:* _____

**93. Where are the erector spinae positioned?**

a) Chest
b) Either side of the spine
c) Top of the scapula
d) Neck

*Answer:* _____

**94. Where is the anconeus positioned?**

a) Forearm
b) Wrist
c) Elbow
d) Shoulder

*Answer:* _____

**95. What is the action of the flexor carpi ulnaris?**

a) Pronates forearm
b) Flexes elbow joint
c) Extends elbow
d) Flexes wrist

*Answer:* _____

**96. Which muscle adducts and medially rotates the thigh?**

a) Vastus lateralis
b) Gastrocnemius
c) Soleus
d) Gracilis

*Answer:* _____

| | |
|---|---|
| **97. Which muscle inverts the foot?**<br><br>a) Extensor digitorum longus<br>b) Tibialis anterior<br>c) Peroneus longus<br>d) Soleus<br><br><br>*Answer:* _____ | **98. Which one of the following is not a function of the muscular system?**<br><br>a) Support<br>b) Movement<br>c) Heat production<br>d) Maintenance of posture<br><br>*Answer:* _____ |
| **99. What is the action of the sartorius?**<br><br>a) Rotates femur medially<br>b) Flexes hip and knee<br>c) Extends hip and knee<br>d) Extends knee<br><br><br>*Answer:* _____ | **100. Which muscle makes up the calf muscle?**<br><br>a) Soleus<br>b) Gracilis<br>c) Peroneus longus<br>d) Gastrocnemius<br><br><br>*Answer:* _____ |
| **101. Lack of tone in a muscle is known as;**<br><br>a) Myositis<br>b) Atony<br>c) Atrophy<br>d) Rupture<br><br><br>*Answer:* _____ | **102. What muscle is positioned at the lateral side of the scapula?**<br><br>a) Infraspinatus<br>b) Supraspinatus<br>c) Teres major<br>d) Serratus anterior<br><br><br>*Answer:* _____ |
| **103. Where is the gluteus minimus positioned?**<br><br>a) Above the gluteus maximus<br>b) Pelvic floor<br>c) Beneath the gluteus medius<br>d) Side of thorax<br><br><br>*Answer:* _____ | **104. What is the position of the flexor carpi ulnaris?**<br><br>a) Upper arm<br>b) Shoulder<br>c) Forearm<br>d) Wrist joint<br><br><br>*Answer:* _____ |
| **105. The levator labii superioris produces which expression?**<br><br>a) Sadness<br>b) Annoying expression<br>c) Disgusted expression<br>d) Smiling<br><br><br>*Answer:* _____ | **106. What is the action of the procerus nasi?**<br><br>a) Wrinkles in between the eyebrows<br>b) Dilates nasal opening<br>c) Lifts upper lip<br>d) Purses lips<br><br><br>*Answer:* _____ |

| | |
|---|---|
| **107. Moving a limb away from the midline is known as;**<br>a) Dorsiflexion<br>b) Flexion<br>c) Abduction<br>d) Extension<br><br>*Answer:* _____ | **108. What direction does a muscle take?**<br>a) From its origin towards its insertion<br>b) From its insertion towards its origin<br>c) From the muscle fibres to the origin<br>d) From the belly of the muscle to its insertion<br><br>*Answer:* _____ |
| **109. What is the action of the anconeus?**<br>a) Flexes wrist joint<br>b) Extends elbow<br>c) Extends wrist joint<br>d) Extends fingers<br><br><br>*Answer:* _____ | **110. What is the position of the supinator radii brevi?**<br>a) Elbow<br>b) Shoulder<br>c) Upper arm<br>d) Forearm<br><br>*Answer:* _____ |
| **111. Which muscle rotates the femur laterally?**<br>a) Peroneus longus<br>b) Vastus lateralis<br>c) Sartorius<br>d) Soleus<br><br>*Answer:* _____ | **112. A tear in the fascia surrounding the muscle is called;**<br>a) Strain<br>b) Sprain<br>c) Rupture<br>d) Fibrositis<br><br>*Answer:* _____ |
| **113. Which muscle is positioned on the front of the lower leg?**<br>a) Extensor digitorum longus<br>b) Peroneus longus<br>c) Gastrocnemius<br>d) Flexor digitorum longus<br><br>*Answer:* _____ | **114. Bending a body part inwards is known as;**<br>a) Adduction<br>b) Flexion<br>c) Extension<br>d) Supination<br><br>*Answer:* _____ |
| **115. Flexing a foot with the toe down and the heel up is known as;**<br>a) Plantarflexion<br>b) Pronation<br>c) Dorsiflexion<br>d) Eversion<br><br>*Answer:* _____ | **116. What is the action of the orbicularis oculi?**<br>a) Opens the eye<br>b) Closes the eye<br>c) Lifts the upper jaw<br>d) Lifts the lower jaw<br><br>*Answer:* _____ |

| | |
|---|---|
| **117. Where is the sternocleidomastoid positioned?**<br>a) Back of the neck<br>b) Shoulders<br>c) Sides of the neck<br>d) Neck to the trunk<br><br>*Answer:* _____ | **118. What is the action of the coracobrachialis?**<br>a) Adducts humerus<br>b) Extends humerus<br>c) Abducts humerus<br>d) Flexes elbow<br><br>*Answer:* _____ |
| **119. What muscle flexes the wrist?**<br>a) Pronator Teres<br>b) Brachioradialis<br>c) Flexor carpi ulnaris<br>d) Extensor carpi ulnaris<br><br><br>*Answer:* _____ | **120. Eversion describes;**<br>a) Bending the foot towards the midline of the body<br>b) Turning the feet to face downwards<br>c) Turning the foot to face outwards<br>d) Bending the foot to face upwards<br><br>*Answer:* _____ |
| **121. Which muscle is positioned on top of the semimembranosus?**<br>a) Gastrocnemius<br>b) Semitendinosus<br>c) Gracilis<br>d) Adductor magnus<br><br>*Answer:* _____ | **122. What is the action of the tibialis anterior?**<br>a) Plantarflexes foot<br>b) Inverts foot<br>c) Plantarflexes and everts foot<br>d) Flexes toes<br><br>*Answer:* _____ |
| **123. What is the position of the vastus lateralis?**<br>a) Medial and front of thigh<br>b) Front of thigh<br>c) Medial side of the knee<br>d) Lateral and front of thigh<br><br>*Answer:* _____ | **124. Which muscle does not extend the hip?**<br>a) Biceps femoris<br>b) Semitendinosus<br>c) Semimembranosus<br>d) Rectus femoris<br><br>*Answer:* _____ |
| **125. Which muscle surrounds the eye?**<br>a) Orbicularis oris<br>b) Levator palpebrae<br>c) Orbicularis oculi<br>d) Temporalis<br><br><br>*Answer:* _____ | **126. What is the action of the anterior deltoid?**<br>a) Draws arm backwards<br>b) Elevates shoulders<br>c) Rotates scapula<br>d) Draws arm forward<br><br>*Answer:* _____ |

| 127. What is the action of the gluteus maximus? | 128. What is the action of the pronator teres? |
|---|---|
| a) Flexes hip<br>b) Rotates thigh medially<br>c) Rotates thigh laterally<br>d) Flexes vertebral column<br><br>Answer: _____ | a) Flexes wrist joint<br>b) Pronates forearm<br>c) Flexes finger<br>d) Extends elbow<br><br>Answer: _____ |
| 129. Which muscle adducts the arm? | 130. What muscle elevates the upper eyelid? |
| a) Latissimus dorsi<br>b) Erector spinae<br>c) Supraspinatus<br>d) Splenius capitis<br><br>Answer: _____ | a) Levator palpebrae<br>b) Masseter<br>c) Orbicularis oculi<br>d) Sternocleidomastoid<br><br>Answer: _____ |
| 131. What is the structure of fascia? | 132. What is the position of the adductor longus? |
| a) Fibrous muscle fibres<br>b) Fibrous connective tissue<br>c) Fibrous elastic tissue<br>d) Fibrous elastic cords<br><br>Answer: _____ | a) Front of the thigh<br>b) Lateral and front of thigh<br>c) Lateral front of lower leg<br>d) Medial side of thigh<br><br>Answer: _____ |
| 133. Which muscle is positioned on the medial and front of the thigh? | 134. What is the action of the extensor carpi radialis? |
| a) Vastus lateralis<br>b) Rectus femoris<br>c) Vastus intermedius<br>d) Vastus medialis<br><br>Answer: _____ | a) Extends fingers<br>b) Extends wrist<br>c) Extends elbow<br>d) Extends forearm<br><br>Answer: _____ |
| 135. What muscle is positioned on the posterior forearm? | 136. Where is the trapezius positioned? |
| a) Brachialis<br>b) Flexor carpi radialis<br>c) Triceps<br>d) Extensor carpi ulnaris<br><br>Answer: _____ | a) Lower back<br>b) Shoulders<br>c) Neck<br>d) Upper back<br><br>Answer: _____ |

| | |
|---|---|
| **137. Which muscle abducts the femur?**<br>a) Gluteus minimus<br>b) Adductor magnus<br>c) Semitendinosus<br>d) Gracilis<br><br><br>*Answer:* _____ | **138. What muscle draws the scapula forward?**<br>a) Sternocleidomastoid<br>b) Serratus anterior<br>c) Pectoralis major<br>d) Deltoid<br><br>*Answer:* _____ |
| **139. What muscle runs from the back of the neck to the upper thorax?**<br>a) Splenius capitis<br>b) Sternocleidomastoid<br>c) Levator scapulae<br>d) Trapezius<br><br>*Answer:* _____ | **140. What is the action of the depressor anguli oris?**<br>a) Raises the mandible<br>b) Retracts lower jaw<br>c) Depression of the corners of the mouth<br>d) Pull down lower lip<br><br>*Answer:* _____ |
| **141. Where is the mentalis positioned?**<br>a) Cheek<br>b) Forehead<br>c) Chin<br>d) Nose<br><br><br><br>*Answer:* _____ | **142. Which muscle is responsible for smiling or laughing?**<br>a) Levator anguli oris<br>b) Zygomaticus<br>c) Buccinator<br>d) Levator labii superioris<br><br>*Answer:* _____ |
| **143. Pointing the foot upwards is known as;**<br>a) Pronation<br>b) Plantarflexion<br>c) Supination<br>d) Dorsiflexion<br><br>*Answer:* _____ | **144. Which muscle is positioned on the posterior forearm?**<br>a) Deltoid<br>b) Biceps<br>c) Coracobrachialis<br>d) Extensor carpi ulnaris<br><br>*Answer:* _____ |
| **145. The moveable end of a muscle is called;**<br>a) The insertion<br>b) The origin<br>c) The attachment<br>d) The belly<br><br>*Answer:* _____ | **146. Where is the nasalis positioned?**<br>a) Above the eyebrows<br>b) Between the upper lip and bottom of nose<br>c) Sides of the nose<br>d) Between the eyebrows<br><br>*Answer:* _____ |

**147. Which muscle is positioned on the chin?**

a) Masseter

b) Zygomaticus

c) Temporalis

d) Depressor anguli oris

*Answer:* _____

**148. What muscle closes the mouth?**

a) Orbicularis oris

b) Levator anguli oris

c) Orbicularis oculi

d) Lateral pterygoid

*Answer:* _____

**149. Which muscles flexes the fingers?**

a) Flexor carpi ulnaris

b) Flexor carpi digitorum

c) Flexor carpi radialis

d) Anconeus

*Answer:* _____

**150. Which muscle is positioned on the outside of the thigh?**

a) Biceps femoris

b) Gracilis

c) Adductor magnus

d) Semimembranosus

*Answer:* _____

**151. Which muscle is responsible for creating a grinning expression?**

a) Temporalis

b) Levator palpebrae

c) Risorius

d) Mentalis

*Answer:* _____

**152. Mastication is another term for;**

a) Grinning

b) Chewing

c) Smiling

d) Sneezing

*Answer:* _____

**153. What is the action of the splenius capitis?**

a) Flexes the head

b) Extends the head

c) Raises shoulders

d) Draws arm backwards

*Answer:* _____

**154. What is the position of the flexor carpi digitorum?**

a) Anterior forearm

b) Posterior forearm

c) Fingers

d) Wrist

*Answer:* _____

**155. What is the action of the biceps femoris?**

a) Extend knee

b) Extend toes

c) Flex hip

d) Flex knee

*Answer:* _____

**156. A disorder of the muscular system;**

a) Hypoglycaemia

b) Fibromyalgia

c) Hodgkin's Disease

d) Arthritis

*Answer:* _____

| | |
|---|---|
| **157. What is the most powerful tendon in the body?**<br>a) Flexor digitorum longus<br>b) Tibialis anterior<br>c) Tendon of achilles<br>d) Sartorius<br><br>*Answer:* _____ | **158. Which muscle is not positioned on the posterior forearm?**<br>a) Flexor carpi radialis<br>b) Extensor carpi ulnaris<br>c) Extensor carpi digitorum<br>d) Supinator<br><br>*Answer:* _____ |
| **159. What is the action of the middle deltoid?**<br>a) Draws arm forward<br>b) Abducts the arm<br>c) Adducts the arm<br>d) Draws arm backward<br><br>*Answer:* _____ | **160. What is the action of the supraspinatus?**<br>a) Abducts humerus<br>b) Rotates humerus medially<br>c) Rotates humerus laterally<br>d) Adducts humerus<br><br>*Answer:* _____ |
| **161. Where are the deltoids positioned?**<br>a) Shoulder<br>b) Arm<br>c) Upper back<br>d) Abdominals<br><br>*Answer:* _____ | **162. The orbicularis oris is positioned;**<br>a) Across the face<br>b) Around the mouth<br>c) Chin<br>d) From the forehead to the nose<br><br>*Answer:* _____ |
| **163. Which one of the following is the main muscle of mastication?**<br>a) Buccinator<br>b) Orbicularis oculi<br>c) Mentalis<br>d) Masseter<br><br>*Answer:* _____ | **164. What muscle works alongside the triceps to extend the elbow?**<br>a) Anconeus<br>b) Biceps<br>c) Teres major<br>d) Deltoid<br><br>*Answer:* _____ |
| **165. What is the position of the masseter?**<br>a) From zygomatic arch to mandible<br>b) Around the eye<br>c) Between masseter and corner of mouth<br>d) Upper eyelid<br><br>*Answer:* _____ | **166. The belly of a muscle describes;**<br>a) The insertion of the muscle<br>b) The fixed end of the muscle<br>c) The contracting muscle<br>d) The thickest section of the muscle<br><br>*Answer:* _____ |

**167. The inability of a muscle to contract efficiently is caused by which one of the following?**

a) Length of a muscle
b) Position of the muscle
c) Thickness of the muscle
d) Lactic acid

Answer: _____

**168. What is the action of the extensor digitorum longus?**

a) Extends toes
b) Flexes toes
c) Abducts foot
d) Plantarflexes foot

Answer: _____

**169. What is the position of the peroneus longus?**

a) Lateral side of the lower leg
b) Posterior lower leg
c) Anterior and medial side of the lower leg
d) Front of the thigh

Answer: _____

**170. What is the action of the extensor carpi digitorum?**

a) Extends fingers
b) Extends elbow
c) Extends wrist
d) Supinates forearm

Answer: _____

**171. What is the action of the gluteus minimus?**

a) Laterally rotates femur
b) Medially rotates femur
c) Laterally rotates hip
d) Medially rotates hip

Answer: _____

**172. Which muscle flexes the humerus?**

a) Biceps
b) Brachioradialis
c) Flexor carpi ulnaris
d) Coracobrachialis

Answer: _____

**173. Which muscle extends the vertebral column?**

a) Internal oblique
b) Transverse abdominus
c) External oblique
d) Erector spinae

Answer: _____

**174. Which muscle medially rotates the arm?**

a) Sternocleidomastoid
b) Deltoid
c) Pectoralis major
d) Serratus anterior

Answer: _____

**175. Which one of the following does not flex the vertebral column?**

a) Internal oblique
b) External oblique
c) Ilio psoas
d) Rectus abdominis

Answer: _____

**176. What type of tissue is fascia composed of?**

a) Fibrous
b) Elastic
c) Yellow elastic
d) Adipose

Answer: _____

**177. Bending a limb outwards is known as;**
a) Abduction
b) Eversion
c) Rotation
d) Extension

*Answer:* _____

**178. Where is the procerus nasi positioned?**
a) Sides of the nose
b) Between eyebrows
c) Lower lip
d) Above the eyebrow

*Answer:* _____

**179. What is the main muscle used when sniffing or blowing the nose?**
a) Procerus nasi
b) Frontalis
c) Masseter
d) Nasalis

*Answer:* _____

**180. Which muscle lifts the upper lip?**
a) Levator labii superioris
b) Zygomaticus
c) Levator palpebrae
d) Splenius capitis

*Answer:* _____

**181. What is the action of the medial pterygoid?**
a) Depresses the lower lip
b) Opens the eyelid
c) Raises the mandible
d) Lowers the corners of the mouth

*Answer:* _____

**182. What does the build up of lactic acid cause?**
a) Muscle fatigue
b) Muscle contraction
c) Muscle relaxation
d) Isometric contraction

*Answer:* _____

**183. What is the position of the sartorius?**
a) Crosses hip to medial side of tibia
b) Crosses hip to lateral side of tibia
c) Crosses from the hip to behind the knee
d) Deep to the adductor brevis

*Answer:* _____

**184. Which muscle extends the knee?**
a) Gracilis
b) Semitendinosus
c) Vastus intermedius
d) Tibialis anterior

*Answer:* _____

**185. Which muscle is positioned on the posterior forearm?**
a) Brachioradialis
b) Extensor carpi digitorum
c) Anconeus
d) Pronator Teres

*Answer:* _____

**186. What is the action of the semitendinosus?**
a) Extends knee
b) Extends hip
c) Flexes hip
d) Extends foot

*Answer:* _____

**187. What muscle is positioned on the lower leg?**

a) Adductor brevis

b) Rectus femoris

c) Flexor digitorum longus

d) Serratus anterior

*Answer: _____*

**188. A build up of lactic acid inside muscles causing pain and stiffness;**

a) Fibrositis

b) Atony

c) Spasm

d) Spasticity

*Answer: _____*

**189. Where is the teres minor positioned?**

a)  Side of scapula

b) Top of scapula

c) Between scapula and spine

d) Below scapula

*Answer: _____*

**190. Which muscle adducts and rotates the thigh laterally?**

a) Gluteus maximus

b) Gluteus minimus

c) Gluteus medius

d) Teres Major

*Answer: _____*

**191. Which muscle adducts the femur?**

a) Gluteus medius

b) Biceps femoris

c) Adductor magnus

d) Sartorius

*Answer: _____*

**192. Where is the gluteus medius positioned?**

a) Lower buttocks

b) Underneath the gluteus minimus

c) Underneath the gluteus maximus

d) Pelvic floor

*Answer: _____*

**193. Where are the internal and external obliques positioned?**

a) Abdominal wall

b) Waist

c) Deep to the abdominal wall

d) Side of scapula

*Answer: _____*

**194. Turning the foot to face inwards;**

a) Inversion

b) Abduction

c) Eversion

d) Extension

*Answer: _____*

**195. Where is the levator labii superioris positioned?**

a) Below the eyebrows

b) Between the eyebrows

c) Cheek

d) Chin

*Answer: _____*

**196. What is the position of the zygomaticus?**

a) Between the chin and lower lip

b) Under the mandible

c) Forehead

d) Cheek

*Answer: _____*

| | |
|---|---|
| **197. Which muscle opens the nostrils?**<br><br>a) Frontalis<br>b) Nasalis<br>c) Levator palpebrae<br>d) Temporalis<br><br><br>*Answer:* _____ | **198. Muscle that relaxes to allow the prime mover to contract;**<br><br>a) The insertion<br>b) The antagonist<br>c) The muscle belly<br>d) The agonist<br><br>*Answer:* _____ |
| **199. What is the action of the adductor magnus?**<br><br>a) Adducts femur<br>b) Abducts femur<br>c) Extends knee<br>d) Flexes knee<br><br><br>*Answer:* _____ | **200. What is the position of the vastus intermedius?**<br><br>a) Posterior thigh<br>b) Front of thigh<br>c) Lateral thigh<br>d) Deep to soleus<br><br><br>*Answer:* _____ |
| **201. What is the action of the supinator radii brevi?**<br><br>a) Extends fingers<br>b) Adducts humerus<br>c) Supinates forearm<br>d) Extends wrist<br><br><br>*Answer:* _____ | **202. What is the position of the semimembranosus?**<br><br>a) Lateral aspect of thigh<br>b) Front of thigh<br>c) Medial aspect of thigh<br>d) Back of thigh<br><br><br>*Answer:* _____ |
| **203. Which muscle flexes the knee?**<br><br>a) Gracilis<br>b) Soleus<br>c) Peroneus longus<br>d) Rectus femoris<br><br><br><br>*Answer:* _____ | **204. What 2 muscles form the tendon of achilles?**<br><br>a) Gracilis and soleus<br>b) Peroneus longus and gracilis<br>c) Soleus and gastrocnemius<br>d) Gastrocnemius and peroneus longus<br><br><br>*Answer:* _____ |
| **205. What is the action of the teres minor?**<br><br>a) Draws arm backwards<br>b) Laterally rotates the humerus<br>c) Draws shoulder forwards<br>d) Medially rotates the humerus<br><br>*Answer:* _____ | **206. What is the action of the rectus abdominis?**<br><br>a) Extends vertebral column<br>b) Rotates femur medially<br>c) Flexes the vertebral column<br>d) Rotates the trunk to each side<br><br>*Answer:* _____ |

**207. Adduction describes;**
a) Moving a limb away from the midline
b) Moving a limb towards the midline
c) Turning a limb to face upwards
d) Turning a limb towards the centre

*Answer:* _____

**208. What is the action of the zygomaticus?**
a) Pulls lower lip down
b) Lifts upper lip
c) Moves angle of mouth upwards and outwards
d) Purses lips

*Answer:* _____

**209. Which muscle is positioned under rectus femoris?**
a) Vastus intermedius
b) Semimembranosus
c) Vastus lateralis
d) Transverse abdominis

*Answer:* _____

**210. Which muscle extends the knee?**
a) Vastus lateralis
b) Semitendinosus
c) Sartorius
d) Biceps femoris

*Answer:* _____

**211. Which muscle plantarflexes the foot?**
a) Soleus
b) Extensor digitorum longus
c) Tibialis anterior
d) Tendon of achilles

*Answer:* _____

**212. What muscle is positioned at the back of the lower leg?**
a) Peroneus longus
b) Gastrocnemius
c) Tibialis anterior
d) Sartorius

*Answer:* _____

**213. What muscle flexes the toes?**
a) Tibialis anterior
b) Flexor digitorum longus
c) Soleus
d) Gracilis

*Answer:* _____

**214. What is the position of the infraspinatus?**
a) Chest
b) Scapula
c) Neck
d) Buttocks

*Answer:* _____

**215. What is the action of the rhomboids?**
a) Draws shoulder forward
b) Abducts arm
c) Adducts scapula
d) Abducts scapula

*Answer:* _____

**216. What is the action of the levator anguli oris?**
a) Lifts the corner of the mouth
b) Lifts upper lip
c) Moves cheek back
d) Raises the mandible

*Answer:* _____

| | |
|---|---|
| **217. What muscle is positioned underneath the gastocnemius?**<br>a) Peroneus longus<br>b) Tibialis anterior<br>c) Soleus<br>d) Extensor digitorum longus<br><br>*Answer:* _____ | **218. What muscle is responsible for walking and standing?**<br>a) Adductor magnus<br>b) Peroneus longus<br>c) Soleus<br>d) Gracilis<br><br>*Answer:* _____ |
| **219. What is the action of the semimembranosus?**<br>a) Flexes toes<br>b) Flexes knee, extends hip<br>c) Extends knee, flexes hip<br>d) Extends foot<br><br>*Answer:* _____ | **220. Which muscle is positioned at the top of the scapula?**<br>a) Subscapularis<br>b) Splenius capitis<br>c) Supraspinatus<br>d) Infraspinatus<br><br>*Answer:* _____ |
| **221. What is the action of the gluteus medius?**<br>a) Adducts thigh<br>b) Rotates thigh medially<br>c) Rotates thigh laterally<br>d) Extends hip<br><br>*Answer:* _____ | **222. Where is the latissimus dorsi positioned?**<br>a) Upper back<br>b) Covers back<br>c) Lower back<br>d) Shoulders<br><br>*Answer:* _____ |
| **223. Where is the serratus anterior positioned?**<br>a) Chest<br>b) Shoulder<br>c) Abdominal wall<br>d) Side of chest<br><br>*Answer:* _____ | **224. Which muscle flexes the trunk?**<br>a) Pectoralis major<br>b) External oblique<br>c) Ilio psoas<br>d) Serratus anterior<br><br>*Answer:* _____ |
| **225. What muscle pulls the lower lip out?**<br>a) Depressor anguli oris<br>b) Masseter<br>c) Medial pterygoid<br>d) Mentalis<br><br>*Answer:* _____ | **226. What is the action of the posterior deltoid?**<br>a) Draws arm backwards<br>b) Lowers scapula<br>c) Adducts humerus<br>d) Adducts leg<br><br>*Answer:* _____ |

**227. Where is the pectoralis major positioned?**

a) Waist

b) Chest

c) Shoulder

d) Arm

Answer: _____

**228. What is the position of the depressor labii inferioris?**

a) Sides of nose

b) Chin

c) Cheek

d) Forehead

Answer: _____

**229. Which one of the following is not an action of the latissimus dorsi?**

a) Draws arm backwards

b) Adducts the arm

c) Rotates the arm medially

d) Abducts the arm

Answer: _____

**230. What is the position of the levator palpebrae?**

a) Between the eyes

b) Chin

c) Deep to the zygomaticus

d) Upper eyelid

Answer: _____

**231. What is lateral epicondylitis?**

a) Golfer's elbow

b) Tennis elbow

c) Shin splints

d) Muscle dystrophy

Answer: _____

**232. What muscle laterally flexes the lumbar vertebrae?**

a) Latissimus dorsi

b) Quadratus lumborum

c) Gluteus maximus

d) Piriformis

Answer: _____

**233. What muscle abducts the thumb?**

a) Abductor pollicis brevis

b) Flexor carpi ulnaris

c) Palmaris longus

d) Anconeus

Answer: _____

**234. What is the action of the peroneus tertius?**

a) Plantarflexes and inverts the foot

b) Dorsiflexes and inverts the foot

c) Dorsiflexes and everts the foot

d) Plantarflexes and everts the foot

Answer: _____

**235. What is the action of the flexor digitorum profundus?**

a) Flexes the thumb

b) Flexes distal phalanges

c) Flexes the hand

d) Flexes the wrist

Answer: _____

**236. What is the action of the flexor pollicis brevis?**

a) Adduction of thumb

b) Abducts little finger

c) Flexion of wrist

d) Abduction of thumb

Answer: _____

| 237. What is the action of the extensor pollicus longus? | 238. What is the term used to describe golfer's elbow? |
|---|---|
| a) Extends wrist | a) Tendonitis |
| b) Flexes wrist | b) Lateral epicondylitis |
| c) Extends thumb | c) Medial epicondylitis |
| d) Extends little finger | d) Bursitis |
| | |
| Answer: _____ | Answer: _____ |

# The Muscular System - Crossword 1

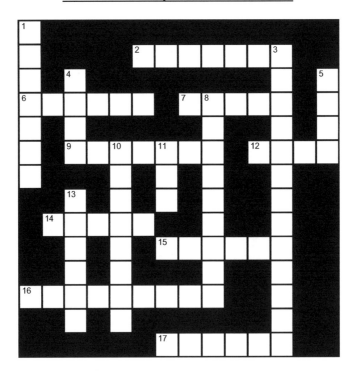

## Across
2. The extensor carpii digitorum extends what part of the body? (7)
6. Involuntary muscle (6)
7. Muscle that flexes the elbow (5)
9. What muscle dilates the nostrils? (7)
12. What part of the body is the levator labii superioris found? (4)
14. The main body of muscle (5)
15. The part of the muscle that does not move (6)
16. A limb facing downwards (9)
17. What muscle plantarflexes the foot? (6)

## Down
1. Over-stimulation of muscle fibres cause? (7)
3. What muscle abducts the arm? (13)
4. How is the toe positioned during plantarflexion? (4)
5. The vastus lateralis extends what part of the body? (4)
8. The moving end of a muscle (9)
10. Another term for voluntary muscle (8)
11. What part of the body is the tibialis anterior located? (3)
13. Connects muscle to bone (6)

# The Muscular System - Crossword 2

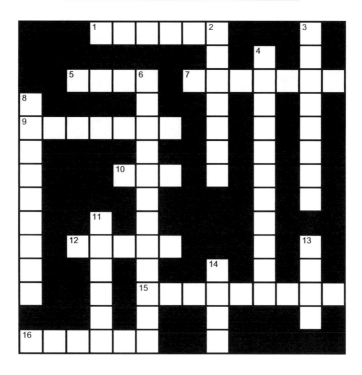

## Across

1. What part of the body does the orbicularis oculi close? (6)
5. The splenius capitis extends what part of the body? (4)
7. A muscle's main fuel (7)
9. Tearing of the fascia (7)
10. What part of the body does the semitendinosus extend? (3)
12. Main composition of muscle (5)
15. Turning the foot towards the centre (9)
16. What can over working a muscle cause? (6)

## Down

2. Shoulder muscle (7)
3. What muscle creates a grinning expression? (8)
4. A muscle which moves scalp backwards (11)
6. Flexing foot up (12)
8. What muscle moves scalp forwards? (9)
11. A type of muscle attachment (6)
13. The achilles tendon plantarflexes which part of the body? (4)
14. The sternocleidomastoid is located in which part of the body? (4)

# The Muscular System - Crossword 3

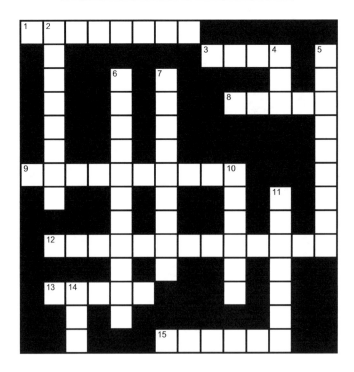

## Across

1. Main muscle of mastication (8)
3. What does the flexor carpi ulnaris adduct? (4)
8. The adductor magnus adducts which part of the body? (5)
9. Thigh muscles (10)
12. Calf muscle (13)
13. The triceps extend which part of the body? (5)
15. _____ Femoris - Muscle which extends the hip (6)

## Down

2. Muscle that extends forearm (8)
4. The pronator teres is positioned on which part of the body? (3)
5. Muscle that flexes hip and knee (9)
6. Muscle movement (11)
7. Movement of a limb towards the midline of the body (9)
10. Muscle responsible for walking (5)
11. Muscle that extends elbow (7)
14. Depressor labii inferioris is responsible for moving which part of the body (3)

# The Muscular System - Crossword 4

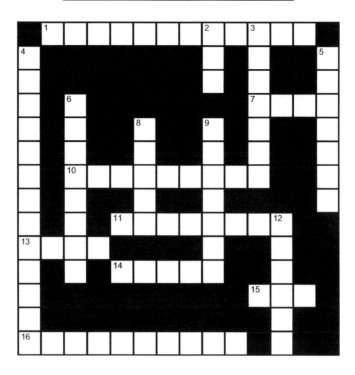

## Across

1. Pain and stiffness in muscles causing lethargy and fatigue (12)
7. Slight contraction of muscle fibres (4)
10. What muscle laterally rotates the femur? (9)
11. Inflammation of a muscle (8)
13. What part of the body does the flexor digitorum longus flex? (4)
14. Where does cardiac muscle exist? (5)
15. Which part of the body is the tibialis anterior positioned? (3)
16. Turning a limb to face upwards (10)

## Down

2. The brachioradialis is located on which part of the body? (3)
3. _____ Maximus (7)
4. Muscle that pronates forearm (13)
5. Bending a body part inwards (7)
6. Skeletal muscle (8)
8. Lack of tension or tone in a muscle (5)
9. Prime mover (7)
12. Muscle positioned underneath the gastrocnemius (6)

## The Muscular System – Crossword 5

**Across**

4. Chest muscle (15)
8. What muscle is positioned on the anterior humerus? (6)
10. What does the flexor carpi ulnaris adduct? (4)
11. What muscle raises the lower jaw? (10)
12. What muscle laterally rotates the humerus? (10)
14. What part of a muscle has little movement during action? (6)
16. A type of muscle movement (7)
18. What muscle adducts the thigh? (14)
19. What muscle compresses the cheek? (10)

**Down**

1. The bending of a body part (7)
2. What can vigorous exercise cause in a muscle? (5)
3. What muscle flexes the forearm at the elbow joint? (10)
5. A type of muscle contraction where the muscle does not actually move (9)
6. Skeletal muscle (9)
7. What muscle plantarflexes and everts the foot? (14)
9. A disorder of the muscular system associated with the nervous system (10)
13. Turing the sole of the foot to face outwards (8)
15. What muscle draws the arm forwards? (7)
17. What does a sudden, sharp twist to the joint cause? (6)

# The Muscular System - Crossword 6

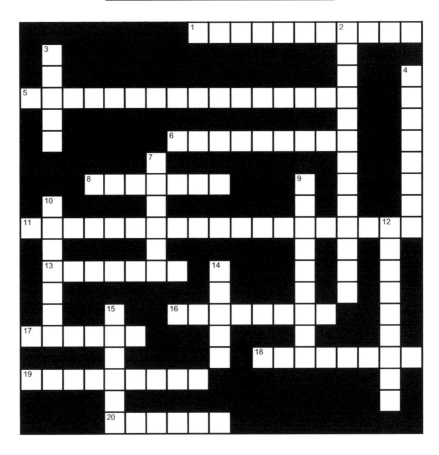

**Across**

1. What muscle is used when smiling? (11)
5. What muscle inverts and dorsiflexes the foot? (16)
6. What muscle adducts the scapula? (9)
8. What muscle is positioned at the sides of the nose? (7)
11. What muscle flexes the wrist? (19)
13. Involuntary muscle found in the wall of the heart (7)
16. Inflammation of a muscle (8)
17. A way in which muscles are attached to the body (6)
18. What muscle is positioned on the chin? (8)
19. What muscle is positioned on the upper back? (9)
20. Involuntary muscle (6)

**Down**

2. What muscle laterally rotates the humerus? (13)
3. What part of the body does the extensor carpi radialis extend? (5)
4. What muscle is positioned at the elbow? (8)
7. A fibrous connective tissue which covers muscles (6)
9. Moving a limb away from the body (9)
10. What provides the muscle fibres with energy? (7)
12. The moving end of a muscle (9)
14. Poor muscle tone (5)
15. What muscle is positioned underneath the gastrocnemius? (6)

## The Muscular System - Crossword 7

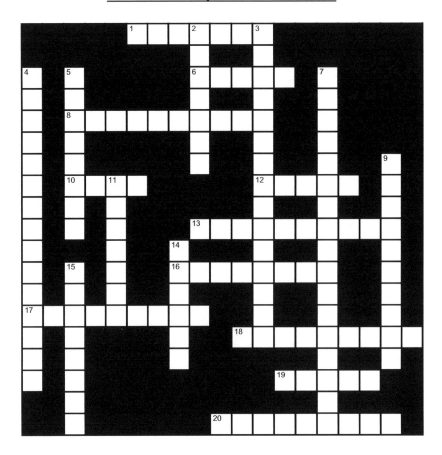

**Across**

1. What part of the arm does the coracobrachialis adduct? (7)
6. What part of the body does the gastrocnemius plantarflex? (5)
8. Facing the palm of the hand upwards (10)
10. What part of the body does the extensor digitorum longus extend? (4)
12. What does an increase in muscle contraction cause? (5)
13. The muscle that does not move while the prime mover is contracting (10)
16. What bone does the lateral pterygoid protract? (8)
17. The opposite of eversion (9)
18. A type of muscle contraction (9)
19. Where in the body is the internal oblique positioned? (5)
20. Straightening of a body part so that the angle between the bones increases (9)

**Down**

2. What type of tissue is a muscle made up of? (7)
3. What muscle extends the head and neck? (15)
4. What muscle flexes the vertebral column? (15)
5. What muscle raises the lower jaw? (8)
7. What muscle extends the knee? (17)
9. What builds up on a muscle when it runs out of oxygen? (10)
11. _____ Spinae (7)
14. What muscle type is not under our conscious control? (6)
15. What do the bones and joints of the skeletal system help the muscular system with? (8)

## Multiple Choice Answers – The Muscular System

| # | Ans | | # | Ans | | # | Ans | | # | Ans | | # | Ans | | # | Ans |
|---|---|---|---|---|---|---|---|---|---|---|---|---|---|---|---|---|---|
| 1 | C | | 41 | C | | 81 | A | | 121 | B | | 161 | A | | 201 | C |
| 2 | C | | 42 | D | | 82 | A | | 122 | B | | 162 | B | | 202 | C |
| 3 | B | | 43 | C | | 83 | C | | 123 | D | | 163 | D | | 203 | A |
| 4 | B | | 44 | B | | 84 | B | | 124 | D | | 164 | A | | 204 | C |
| 5 | C | | 45 | A | | 85 | B | | 125 | C | | 165 | A | | 205 | B |
| 6 | A | | 46 | A | | 86 | A | | 126 | D | | 166 | D | | 206 | C |
| 7 | D | | 47 | C | | 87 | A | | 127 | C | | 167 | D | | 207 | B |
| 8 | C | | 48 | B | | 88 | C | | 128 | B | | 168 | A | | 208 | C |
| 9 | D | | 49 | B | | 89 | D | | 129 | A | | 169 | A | | 209 | A |
| 10 | B | | 50 | A | | 90 | A | | 130 | A | | 170 | A | | 210 | A |
| 11 | A | | 51 | A | | 91 | D | | 131 | B | | 171 | B | | 211 | A |
| 12 | D | | 52 | C | | 92 | A | | 132 | D | | 172 | D | | 212 | B |
| 13 | D | | 53 | D | | 93 | B | | 133 | D | | 173 | D | | 213 | B |
| 14 | D | | 54 | A | | 94 | C | | 134 | B | | 174 | C | | 214 | B |
| 15 | B | | 55 | D | | 95 | D | | 135 | D | | 175 | C | | 215 | C |
| 16 | C | | 56 | D | | 96 | D | | 136 | D | | 176 | A | | 216 | A |
| 17 | C | | 57 | C | | 97 | B | | 137 | A | | 177 | D | | 217 | C |
| 18 | C | | 58 | B | | 98 | A | | 138 | B | | 178 | B | | 218 | C |
| 19 | A | | 59 | A | | 99 | B | | 139 | A | | 179 | D | | 219 | B |
| 20 | D | | 60 | D | | 100 | D | | 140 | C | | 180 | A | | 220 | C |
| 21 | D | | 61 | B | | 101 | B | | 141 | C | | 181 | C | | 221 | B |
| 22 | B | | 62 | A | | 102 | C | | 142 | B | | 182 | A | | 222 | B |
| 23 | D | | 63 | B | | 103 | C | | 143 | D | | 183 | A | | 223 | D |
| 24 | D | | 64 | C | | 104 | C | | 144 | D | | 184 | C | | 224 | B |
| 25 | D | | 65 | D | | 105 | D | | 145 | A | | 185 | B | | 225 | D |
| 26 | A | | 66 | B | | 106 | A | | 146 | C | | 186 | B | | 226 | A |
| 27 | C | | 67 | C | | 107 | C | | 147 | D | | 187 | C | | 227 | B |
| 28 | C | | 68 | A | | 108 | B | | 148 | A | | 188 | A | | 228 | B |
| 29 | D | | 69 | C | | 109 | B | | 149 | B | | 189 | A | | 229 | D |
| 30 | D | | 70 | B | | 110 | D | | 150 | A | | 190 | A | | 230 | D |
| 31 | B | | 71 | C | | 111 | C | | 151 | C | | 191 | C | | 231 | B |
| 32 | C | | 72 | A | | 112 | C | | 152 | B | | 192 | C | | 232 | B |
| 33 | C | | 73 | D | | 113 | A | | 153 | B | | 193 | B | | 233 | A |
| 34 | A | | 74 | C | | 114 | B | | 154 | A | | 194 | A | | 234 | C |
| 35 | B | | 75 | B | | 115 | A | | 155 | D | | 195 | C | | 235 | B |
| 36 | C | | 76 | D | | 116 | B | | 156 | B | | 196 | D | | 236 | D |
| 37 | D | | 77 | D | | 117 | C | | 157 | C | | 197 | B | | 237 | C |
| 38 | B | | 78 | B | | 118 | A | | 158 | A | | 198 | B | | 238 | C |
| 39 | A | | 79 | B | | 119 | C | | 159 | B | | 199 | A | | | |
| 40 | C | | 80 | D | | 120 | C | | 160 | A | | 200 | B | | | |

# Crossword Answers – The Muscular System

## Crossword 1

| Across | Down |
| --- | --- |
| 2. Fingers | 1. Tension |
| 6. Smooth | 3. Supraspinatus |
| 7. Bice p | 4. Down |
| 9. Nasalis | 5. Knee |
| 12. Face | 8. Insertion |
| 14. Belly | 10. Skeletal |
| 15. Origin | 11. Leg |
| 16. Pronation | 13. Tendon |
| 17. Soleus | |

## Crossword 2

| Across | Down |
| --- | --- |
| 1. Eyelid | 2. Deltoid |
| 5. Head | 3. Risorius |
| 7. Glucose | 4. Occipitalis |
| 9. Rupture | 6. Dorsiflexion |
| 10. Hip | 8. Frontalis |
| 12. Water | 11. Fascia |
| 15. Inversion | 13. Foot |
| 16. Strain | 14. Neck |

## Crossword 3

| Across | Down |
| --- | --- |
| 1. Masseter | 2. Anconeus |
| 3. Ulna | 4. Arm |
| 8. Femur | 5. Sartorius |
| 9. Quadriceps | 6. Contraction |
| 12. Gastrocnemius | 7. Adduction |
| 13. Elbow | 10. Soleus |
| 15. Biceps | 11. Triceps |
| | 14. Lip |

## Crossword 4

| Across | Down |
| --- | --- |
| 1. Fibromyalgia | 2. Arm |
| 7. Tone | 3. Gluteus |
| 10. Ilio psoas | 4. Pronator Teres |
| 11. Myositis | 5. Flexion |
| 13. Toes | 6. Striated |
| 14. Heart | 8. Atony |
| 15. Leg | 9. Agonist |
| 16. Supination | 12. Soleus |

## Crossword 5

| Across | Down |
| --- | --- |
| 4. Pectoralis Major | 1. Flexion |
| 8. Biceps | 2. Cramp |
| 10. Ulna | 3. Brachialis |
| 11. Temporalis | 5. Isometric |
| 12. Teres Minor | 6. Voluntary |
| 14. Origin | 7. Peroneus Longus |
| 16. Agonist | 9. Spasticity |
| 18. Adductor Magnus | 13. Eversion |
| 19. Buccinator | 15. Deltoid |
| | 17. Sprain |

## Crossword 6

| Across | Down |
| --- | --- |
| 1. Zygomaticus | 2. Infraspinatus |
| 5. Tibialis Anterior | 3. Wrist |
| 6. Rhomboids | 4. Anconeus |
| 8. Nasalis | 7. Fascia |
| 11. Flexor Carpi Radialis | 9. Abduction |
| 13. Cardiac | 10. Glucose |
| 16. Myositis | 12. Insertion |
| 17. Tendon | 14. Atony |
| 18. Mentalis | 15. Soleus |
| 19. Trapezius | |
| 20. Smooth | |

## Crossword 7

**Across**

1. Humerus
6. Ankle
8. Supination
10. Toes
12. Spasm
13. Antagonist
16. Mandible
17. Inversion
18. Isometric
19. Waist
20. Extension

**Down**

2. Elastic
3. Splenius Capitis
4. Rectus Abdominis
5. Masseter
7. Vastus Intermedius
9. Lactic Acid
11. Erector
14. Smooth
15. Leverage

# Chapter 5 | The Cardiovascular System

## Multiple Choice Questions

| | |
|---|---|
| **1. The outer layer of the heart is called the;**<br>a) Pericardium<br>b) Myocardium<br>c) Sino artrial<br>d) Endocardium<br><br>*Answer:* _____ | **2. Where do capillaries branch from?**<br>a) Arterioles<br>b) Arteries<br>c) Venules<br>d) Veins<br><br><br><br>*Answer:* _____ |
| **3. What is the function of thrombocytes?**<br>a) Transport nutrients in the blood<br>b) Protect the body from infection<br>c) To clot the blood<br>d) Solvent in the blood<br><br><br>*Answer:* _____ | **4. Erythrocytes are;**<br>a) Cells that fight infection<br>b) Cells that transport oxygen as oxyhaemoglobin around the body<br>c) Cells responsible for blood clotting<br>d) Cells that form collagen<br><br>*Answer:* _____ |
| **5. When you are looking at a diagram of the heart, the upper left chamber is called the;**<br>a) Left ventricle<br>b) Right atria<br>c) Right ventricle<br>d) Left atria<br><br><br><br>*Answer:* _____ | **6. The function of monocytes is to;**<br>a) Destroy harmful blood cells to protect the body from infection<br>b) Transport oxygen as oxyhaemoglobin around the body<br>c) Defend the system against micro-organisms<br>d) Eat bacteria and other micro-organisms<br><br>*Answer:* _____ |
| **7. What artery supplies the head and neck?**<br>a) The carotid arteries<br>b) Sphenic artery<br>c) Maxillary artery<br>d) Jugular artery<br><br><br>*Answer:* _____ | **8. Hypertension is another term for;**<br>a) Low blood pressure<br>b) High blood pressure<br>c) Heart attack<br>d) Angina<br><br><br><br>*Answer:* _____ |

| | |
|---|---|
| **9. What is the function of leucocytes?**<br><br>a) Blood clotting<br>b) To fight infection<br>c) To transport waste products<br>d) Regulate body temperature<br><br><br><br><br><br>*Answer:* _____ | **10. The four plasma proteins are as follows;**<br><br>a) Albumin, globulin, fibrinogen and prothrombin<br>b) Potassium, globulin, albumin and prothrombin<br>c) Albumin, potassium, fibrinogen and prothrombin<br>d) Iodine, prothrombin, fibrinogen and albumin<br><br>*Answer:* _____ |
| **11. Where are lymphocytes formed?**<br><br>a) Red bone marrow<br>b) Lymphatic tissue<br>c) Spleen<br>d) Brain<br><br><br>*Answer:* _____ | **12. The middle layer of the heart is called;**<br><br>a) Myocardium<br>b) Pericardium<br>c) Septum<br>d) Endocardium<br><br><br>*Answer:* _____ |
| **13. The action of the heart is controlled by;**<br><br>a) The central nervous system<br>b) The autonomic nervous system<br>c) The spinal cord<br>d) The peripheral nervous system<br><br>*Answer:* _____ | **14. Which layer of the heart contains cardiac muscle?**<br><br>a) Pericardium<br>b) Septum<br>c) Myocardium<br>d) Endocardium<br><br><br>*Answer:* _____ |
| **15. Blood returns from the lungs into which heart chamber?**<br><br>a) Left atria<br>b) Left ventricle<br>c) Right atria<br>d) Right ventricle<br><br>*Answer:* _____ | **16. The blood is pushed from the left atrium into the left ventricle through;**<br><br>a) Micuspid valve<br>b) Tricuspid valve<br>c) Bicuspid valve<br>d) Septum<br><br>*Answer:* _____ |

| | |
|---|---|
| **17. The pulmonary artery;**<br>a) Carries deoxygenated blood from the heart to the lungs<br>b) Carries oxygenated blood to the lungs<br>c) Carry deoxygenated blood from the heart to the body<br>d) Carry oxygenated blood from the heart to the body<br><br>*Answer:* _____ | **18. The function of capillaries include;**<br>a) To deliver oxygen and nutrients to most parts of the body<br>b) To carry deoxygenated blood from the capillaries to the larger veins<br>c) To relax and dilate providing a small blood supply to vital organs<br>d) To carry oxygenated blood to larger veins<br><br>*Answer:* _____ |
| **19. Which one of the following is one of the main arteries of the head and neck?**<br>a) Right renal artery<br>b) Hepatic artery<br>c) Maxillary<br>d) External carotid<br><br>*Answer:* _____ | **20. A haemorrhage occurs when;**<br>a) A capillary bleeds<br>b) No blood clot forms<br>c) A blood clot is formed<br>d) There is high blood pressure<br><br><br>*Answer:* _____ |
| **21. What type of blood can be given to patients with any blood group?**<br>a) Type AB<br>b) Type A<br>c) Type B<br>d) Type O<br><br>*Answer:* _____ | **22. Anaemia can be defined as follows;**<br>a) A reduction in red blood cells<br>b) A reduction in white blood cells<br>c) An increase in the production of erythrocytes<br>d) The inability of the blood to clot<br><br>*Answer:* _____ |
| **23. Inflammation of veins in the rectum;**<br>a) Haemorrhoids<br>b) Amenorrhoea<br>c) Emphysema<br>d) Rhinitis<br><br>*Answer:* _____ | **24. A cancer of the blood is;**<br>a) Septicaemia<br>b) Leukaemia<br>c) Anaemia<br>d) Thrombus<br><br>*Answer:* _____ |
| **25. Hepatitis A, B & C affect which organ of the body;**<br>a) Spleen<br>b) Pancreas<br>c) Heart<br>d) Liver<br><br>*Answer:* _____ | **26. Which body system works with the circulatory system to carry oxygen to the cells and systems of the body?**<br>a) Muscular<br>b) Skeletal<br>c) Respiratory<br>d) Nervous<br><br>*Answer:* _____ |

| | |
|---|---|
| **27. Where are the erythrocytes broken down?**<br>a) In the pancreas<br>b) In the kidneys<br>c) In the lymph<br>d) In the spleen<br><br>*Answer:* _____ | **28. What is the structure of arteries?**<br>a) They have thick muscular walls and a small lumen<br>b) They have thin muscular  walls and a small lumen<br>c) They have thin muscular walls and a thin lumen<br>d) They have thin elastic walls and a large lumen<br><br>*Answer:* _____ |
| **29. Which of the following is caused by a decrease in red blood cells?**<br>a) Anaemia<br>b) Leukaemia<br>c) Atherosclerosis<br>d) Haemorrhoids<br><br>*Answer:* _____ | **30. Which chamber of the heart does oxygenated blood return to?**<br>a) Right atrium<br>b) Left atrium<br>c) Right ventricle<br>d) Left ventricle<br><br>*Answer:* _____ |
| **31. Pulmonary circulation is the transport of blood;**<br>a) From the lungs to the heart<br>b) From the heart to the upper and lower body<br>c) From the heart to the lungs<br>d) From the lungs to the heart and back again<br><br>*Answer:* _____ | **32. Another term for a heartbeat is;**<br>a) Systolic pressure<br>b) Diastolic pressure<br>c) Cardiac cycle<br>d) Pulse<br><br><br><br>*Answer:* _____ |
| **33. What is the main artery that supplies blood to the legs?**<br>a) Tibial<br>b) Renal<br>c) Brachial<br>d) Thrombus<br><br>*Answer:* _____ | **34. What protein gives blood its red colour?**<br>a) Fibrinogen<br>b) Haemoglobin<br>c) Albumin<br>d) Platelets<br><br>*Answer:* _____ |

| | |
|---|---|
| **35. Which one of the following is a type of white blood cell?**<br><br>a) Granulocytes<br>b) Erythrocytes<br>c) Histiocytes<br>d) Thrombocytes<br><br><br>*Answer:* _____ | **36. Systemic circulation is the transport of blood;**<br><br>a) From the heart to the lungs<br>b) From the lungs to the heart<br>c) From the heart to the body<br>d) From the lungs to the rest of the body<br><br>*Answer:* _____ |
| **37. Which chamber of the heart does the heartbeat begin?**<br>a) Left ventricle<br>b) Right atrium<br>c) Right ventricle<br>d) Left Atrium<br><br><br>*Answer:* _____ | **38. Blood is carried to the lungs via tiny vessels called;**<br>a) Capillaries<br>b) Venules<br>c) Arteries<br>d) Arterioles<br><br><br>*Answer:* _____ |
| **39. A function of arterioles;**<br>a) To carry oxygenated blood to the lungs<br>b) To distribute essential waste and bacteria to the body<br>c) To carry deoxygenated blood from the capillaries to the larger veins<br>d) To relax and dilate, speeding up blood flow to the body when needed<br><br><br>*Answer:* _____ | **40. Define interstitial fluid;**<br>a) Fluid which helps to maintain blood pressure<br>b) Fluid which filters out through the capillary walls and bathes the body's tissues<br>c) Fluid that supplies oxygen and nutrients to most parts of the body<br>d) Fluid that helps to maintain body temperature<br><br><br>*Answer:* _____ |
| **41. Which one of the following is one of the main veins of the head and neck?**<br>a) Axillary<br>b) Maxillary<br>c) Internal carotid<br>d) Left iliac vein<br><br><br>*Answer:* _____ | **42. A sphygmomanometer is used for;**<br>a) Measuring plasma content<br>b) Measuring body temperature<br>c) Measuring the level of erythrocytes<br>d) Measuring blood pressure<br><br><br><br><br>*Answer:* _____ |

| | |
|---|---|
| **43. Which of the following is not needed for a blood clot to form?**<br>a) Fibrin<br>b) Vitamin D<br>c) Calcium<br>d) Prothrombin<br><br><br><br><br>*Answer:* _____ | **44. What is the rhesus factor?**<br>a) An antigen found in white blood cells<br>b) An antigen found in red blood cells of most people<br>c) An antigen found in white blood cells of all animals<br>d) An antigen found on the surface of red blood cells in most people and animals<br><br>*Answer:* _____ |
| **45. Which one of the following is not a cause of varicose veins?**<br>a) Pregnancy<br>b) Atherosclerosis<br>c) Obesity<br>d) Heredity<br><br><br>*Answer:* _____ | **46. Haemophilia is another term for;**<br>a) A blood clot in the heart or vessels<br>b) Blood poisoning<br>c) Cancer of the blood<br>d) The inability of the blood to clot<br><br><br><br>*Answer:* _____ |
| **47. AIDS stands for;**<br>a) Acquired immune deficiency syndrome<br>b) Acquired immune disease syndrome<br>c) Anaemic immune disease syndrome<br>d) Anaemic immune deficiency syndrome<br><br><br><br>*Answer:* _____ | **48. Hepatitis A is spread by;**<br>a) Infected blood<br>b) Infected body fluids<br>c) Fecally contaminated food, milk or water<br>d) High cholesterol<br><br><br><br>*Answer:* _____ |
| **49. What is the relationship between the circulatory and skeletal systems?**<br>a) Erythrocytes are produced in the red bone marrow of short bones<br>b) Thrombocytes are produced in the bone marrow of short bones<br>c) Erythrocytes are produced in the bone marrow of long bones<br>d) Erythrocytes are produced in sesamoid bones<br><br>*Answer:* _____ | **50. Coronary thrombosis is defined as;**<br>a) Obstruction of blood flow in the heart<br>b) Obstruction of blood flow in the arteries<br>c ) Obstruction of blood flow in the veins<br>d) Obstruction of blood flow in the coronary artery<br><br><br><br><br>*Answer:* _____ |

| | |
|---|---|
| **51. The inner layer of the heart wall is called;**<br>a) Sino-artrial<br>b) Myocardium<br>c) Endocardium<br>d) Pericardium<br><br><br><br>*Answer:* _____ | **52. What is atherosclerosis?**<br>a) Loss of elasticity in the arterial walls causing a decrease in blood pressure<br>b) Blood poisoning<br>c) Low blood pressure<br>d) A build up of fats inside the arteries causing them to narrow and harden, limiting blood flow to the body<br><br>*Answer:* _____ |
| **53. What is the function of venules?**<br>a) To allow deoxygenated blood to travel from the capillaries to the veins<br>b) To allow deoxygenated blood to travel from the veins to the capillaries<br>c) To allow oxygenated blood to travel from the capillaries to the veins<br>d) To allow oxygenated blood from the veins to the capillaries<br><br>*Answer:* _____ | **54. Which one of the following is not transmitted by infected body fluids such as blood or plasma?**<br>a) Hepatitis B<br>b) Hepatitis C<br>c) Hepatitis A<br>d) Hepatitis C & B<br><br><br><br><br>*Answer:* _____ |
| **55. What is haemophilia?**<br>a) An enlarged vein in the rectum<br>b) A blood clot<br>c) The blood's inability to clot<br>d) Inflammation of a vein<br><br><br><br>*Answer:* _____ | **56. As you look at the diagram of the heart what is the top right hand chamber called?**<br>a) Right atrium<br>b) Left atrium<br>c) Right ventricle<br>d) Left ventricle<br><br><br>*Answer:* _____ |
| **57. Plasma is described as;**<br>a) A pale opaque fluid<br>b) An opaque colourless fluid<br>c) A straw coloured clear liquid<br>d) A bluish white coloured liquid<br><br><br>*Answer:* _____ | **58. What is the wall that separates the right and left sides of the heart called?**<br>a) Pericardium<br>b) Endocardium<br>c) Myocardium<br>d) Septum<br><br><br>*Answer:* _____ |

| | |
|---|---|
| **59. Deoxygenated blood travels;**<br>a) From the heart to the lungs via the pulmonary vein<br>b) From the lungs to the heart via the pulmonary artery<br>c) From the heart to the lungs via the pulmonary artery<br>d) From the lungs to the heart via the pulmonary vein<br><br>*Answer:* _____ | **60. Diastolic relates to;**<br>a) When the heart is contracting<br>b) When the heart is in a period of relaxation<br>c) When the heart is pumping blood around the body<br>d) High blood pressure<br><br>*Answer:* _____ |
| **61. The arteries and veins of the arm and hand include;**<br>a) Digital & saphenous<br>b) Cephalic & basilic<br>c) Median & peronial<br>d) Sciatic & humeral<br><br>*Answer:* _____ | **62. What is thrombosis?**<br>a) The inability of blood to clot<br>b) A blood clot inside a venule<br>c) A blood clot inside a blood vessel<br>d) A blood clot in the arm<br><br>*Answer:* _____ |
| **63. Which plasma protein changes fibrinogen into fibrin?**<br>a) Albumin<br>b) Thrombin<br>c) Adrenaline<br>d) Thromboplastin<br><br>*Answer:* _____ | **64. Patients with which blood type can receive any blood group?**<br>a) Type O<br>b) Type A<br>c) Type AB<br>d) Type B<br><br>*Answer:* _____ |
| **65. Which one of the following is not a cause of anaemia?**<br>a) Severe loss of blood<br>b) Lack of iron in the diet<br>c) Lack of vitamin D in the diet<br>d) Heredity<br><br>*Answer:* _____ | **66. What is the term for blood poisoning?**<br>a) Thrombus<br>b) Phlebitis<br>c) Septicaemia<br>d) Haemophilia<br><br>*Answer:* _____ |

**67. What is the main function of insulin?**
a) Helps the body cells convert excess glucose into glycogen
b) Helps to maintain the correct body temperature
c) Helps the body to burn fat for energy
d) Helps the body to produce erythrocytes

*Answer:* _____

**68. Hepatitis B & C are transmitted by;**
a) Poisonous food
b) Infected body fluids except blood
c) Infected red blood cells
d) Infected body fluids including blood

*Answer:* _____

**69. The lymphatic system works with the circulatory system by;**
a) Transporting waste products away from the tissues
b) Carrying hormones to various organs
c) Carrying oxygen to every cell of the body
d) Transporting oxygen and nutrients to the organs of the body

*Answer:* _____

**70. What is the process by which oxygen can enter the bloodstream?**
a) Absorption
b) Diffusion
c) Osmosis
d) Filtration

*Answer:* _____

**71. Enzymes are described as;**
a) Proteins that speed up the rate of chemical reactions
b) Chemical substances in the body
c) Oxygen and carbon dioxide
d) Chemical messengers in the blood

*Answer:* _____

**72. Where are erythrocytes produced?**
a) Nucleus of a cell
b) Red bone marrow
c) Liver
d) Spleen

*Answer:* _____

**73. How is the process known as phagocytosis defined?**
a) The process of blood clotting
b) The transport of oxygen
c) The process the human body uses to destroy harmful bacteria and other micro organisms
d) The process of producing phagocytes and leucocytes

*Answer:* _____

**74. Systole relates to;**
a) The period of time when the heart is contracting
b) The heartbeat
c) The period of time when the heart is relaxing
d) The pulse

*Answer:* _____

| **75. Deoxygenated blood travels from the upper body into the right atrium via;**<br>a) Pulmonary veins<br>b) Superior vena cava<br>c) Pulmonary artery<br>d) Inferior vena cava<br><br>*Answer: _____* | **76. Arteries carry;**<br>a) Deoxygenated blood to the lungs<br>b) Oxygenated blood to the lungs<br>c) Deoxygenated blood from the heart<br>d) Oxygenated blood from the heart<br><br>*Answer: _____* |
| --- | --- |
| **77. Which one of the following is one of the main veins of the legs?**<br>a) Brachial<br>b) Cephalic<br>c) Axillary<br>d) Anterior tibial<br><br>*Answer: _____* | **78. Hypotension is also known as;**<br>a) Low blood pressure<br>b) High blood pressure<br>c) Blood clotting<br>d) Anaemia<br><br><br>*Answer: _____* |
| **79. Leukaemia is caused by;**<br>a) Abnormal multiplication of white blood cells<br>b) Over production of red blood cells<br>c) A decrease in the multiplication of white blood cells<br>d) A decrease in the multiplication of red blood cells<br><br>*Answer: _____* | **80. Inflammation of a vein is known as;**<br>a) Thrombus<br>b) Haemophilia<br>c) Phlebitis<br>d) Atherosclerosis<br><br><br><br><br><br>*Answer: _____* |
| **81. What blood type is the universal donor?**<br>a) Type AB<br>b) Type O<br>c) Type A<br>d) Type B<br><br>*Answer: _____* | **82. What are the 2 categories of leucocytes?**<br>a) Monocytes and granulocytes<br>b) Lymphocytes and thrombocytes<br>c) Granulocytes and agranulocytes<br>d) Granulocytes and phagocytes<br><br>*Answer: _____* |
| **83. Blood travels from the right ventricle to the lungs via;**<br>a) Pulmonary vein<br>b) Pulmonary artery<br>c) Aorta<br>d) Superior vena cava<br><br>*Answer: _____* | **84. Deoxygenated blood travels from the lower body into the right atrium via;**<br>a) Pulmonary artery<br>b) Pulmonary vein<br>c) Superior vena cava<br>d) Inferior vena cava<br><br>*Answer: _____* |

| | |
|---|---|
| **85. The blood is pushed from the right atrium into the right ventricle through;**<br>a) Micuspid valve<br>b) Tricuspid valve<br>c) Septum valve<br>d) Bicuspid valve<br><br>*Answer:* _____ | **86. What do most venules unite to form?**<br>a) Arteries<br>b) Ventricles<br>c) Capillaries<br>d) Veins<br><br><br>*Answer:* _____ |
| **87. Thrombus is;**<br>a) Inflammation of a vein<br>b) A blood clot in the heart or blood vessels<br>c) Blood poisoning<br>d) Cancer of the blood<br><br>*Answer:* _____ | **88. The pulmonary vein carries blood;**<br>a) From the lungs to the heart<br>b) From the heart to the rest of the body<br>c) From the heart to the lungs<br>d) From the heart to the upper body<br><br><br>*Answer:* _____ |
| **89. Diabetes effects which organ of the body?**<br>a) Liver<br>b) Spleen<br>c) Pancreas<br>d) Lungs<br><br>*Answer:* _____ | **90. Veins carry;**<br>a) Oxygenated blood to the heart<br>b) Oxygenated blood from the lungs to the heart<br>c) Deoxygenated blood to the heart<br>d) Deoxygenated blood to the lungs<br><br>*Answer:* _____ |
| **91. What is tachycardia?**<br>a) A heart pain caused by lack of oxygen to the heart<br>b) A blockage in the pulmonary artery<br>c) A blood clot in the coronary artery<br>d) A particularly rapid heartbeat<br><br>*Answer:* _____ | **92. What is the term for nosebleeds?**<br>a) Epistaxis<br>b) Palpitations<br>c) Bradycardia<br>d) Gangrene<br><br><br>*Answer:* _____ |

# The Cardiovascular System - Crossword 1

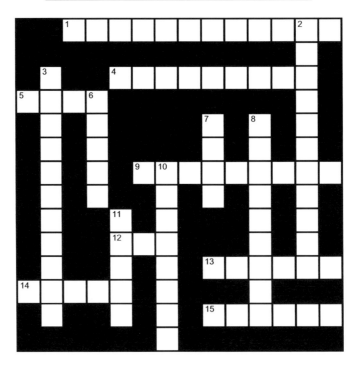

**Across**

1. Red blood cells (12)
4. Valve on the right side of the heart which ensures that blood flows in the right direction (9)
5. Hypertension is another term for what type of blood pressure? (4)
9. Vein of the head and neck (9)
12. A factor that changes the heart rate (3)
13. A slightly thick straw coloured fluid (6)
14. The rate at which your heart is pumping blood through your circulatory system (5)
15. What replaces carbon dioxide in the lungs? (6)

**Down**

2. The inner layer of the heart's wall (10)
3. Part of the heart receives deoxygenated blood from the superior and inferior vena cava? (11)
6. Organ which keeps the blood circulating around the body (5)
7. The pulmonary _____ brings oxygenated blood into the left atrium (4)
8. Type of circulation is involved with the transport of blood from the heart to the lungs? (9)
10. Blood vessels which carry blood away from the heart (8)
11. Plasma carries this substance around the body (5)

## The Cardiovascular System - Crossword 2

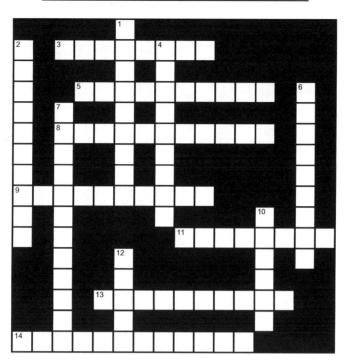

**Across**

3. Valve on the left side of the heart (7)
5. The middle layer of the heart's wall (9)
8. Low blood pressure (11)
9. White blood cells (10)
11. Vein of the arm (8)
13. Blood vessels which deliver blood to the capillaries (10)
14. Heartbeat (12)

**Down**

1. What part of the nervous system controls the actions of the heart? (9)
2. The heart's lower chambers (10)
4. Thrombocytes (9)
6. Inflammation of a vein (9)
7. Antigen found in the red blood cells of most people and animals (12)
10. What is the direction of blood maintained by? (6)
12. The largest artery in the body (5)

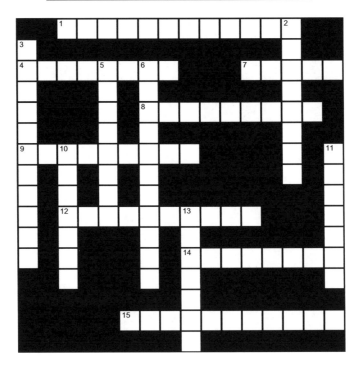

**Across**

1. Cells involved in blood clotting (12)
4. A factor which changes the heart rate (8)
7. Plasma transports this substance to the liver for breakdown (5)
8. Heartbeat starts at a point in the right atrium (9)
9. Aorta which delivers oxygen and nutrients to the upper body (9)
12. What type of blood is received by the left atrium? (10)
14. An artery of the arm (8)
15. Smallest blood vessels (11)

**Down**

2. The circulation of blood from the heart to the body (8)
3. The outer layer of the heart's wall (11)
5. The heart's own circulatory system (8)
6. Blood poisoning (11)
10. Artery of the head and neck (7)
11. Contraction of the heart (7)
13. A plasma protein (7)

# The Cardiovascular System - Crossword 4

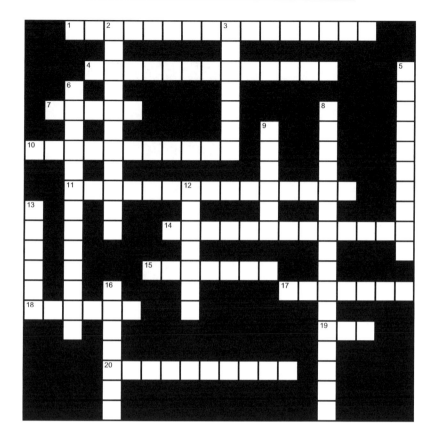

**Across**

1. What is blood pressure measured with? (16)
4. Oxygenated blood leaves the aorta through which chamber of the heart? (13)
7. A fluid connective tissue which carries oxygen, nutrients, hormones and waste materials to and from the cells (5)
10. A plasma protein (11)
11. What takes deoxygenated blood from the heart to the lungs? (15)
14. What do the lungs remove from deoxygenated blood? (13)
15. Artery and vein of the leg (7)
17. A substance needed to form a blood clot (7)
18. Membrane of the inner layer of the pericardium (6)
19. What type of blood cells are erythrocytes? (3)
20. What type of blood cells protect the body against disease? (10)

**Down**

2. A disorder in which the blood clots very slowly (11)

3. What is found in the walls of red blood cells? (7)

5. Chemicals which protect the body by destroying harmful bacteria (10)

6. The amount of pressure that the blood exerts on the arterial walls (13)

8. The hardening of the arteries, limiting the flow of blood through the vessel (16)

9. A substance which is necessary for a clot to form (6)

12. What does a low level of haemoglobin in the blood cause? (7)

13. What type of blood is received by the right atrium through the superior and inferior vena cavae? (6)

16. Vein of the head and neck (7)

# The Cardiovascular System - Crossword 5

**Across**

3. High blood pressure (12)
4. Blood pressure which is below normal (3)
5. What vessels carry blood towards the heart? (5)
8. What blood type can receive blood from any blood group? (6)
9. What type of blood travels from the heart to the lungs in the pulmonary artery? (12)
11. What type of blood cells contain haemoglobin? (12)
14. What vessels eventually join up to form venules? (11)
16. The build up of cholesterol on arteries causing a decrease of blood flow to the heart (15)
17. A substance which is needed for a clot to form (8)
18. What type of epithelial tissue is found in the heart? (8)
19. Vein found in the arm (7)
20. A substance found in plasma (7)

**Down**

1. A condition which produces a blood clot (10)
2. A tissue fluid which provides the cells with oxygen and nutrients (12)
6. A cancer of the blood caused by the over production of white blood cells (9)
7. What type of muscle pushes blood through veins? (8)
10. What gives blood its red colour? (14)
12. Artery and vein of the head and neck (9)
13. A muscular wall which separates the right side of the heart from the left side (6)
15. What organ of the body does hepatitis affect? (5)

## Multiple Choice Answers – The Cardiovascular System

| | | | | | | | | | | | | |
|---|---|---|---|---|---|---|---|---|---|---|---|---|
| 1 | A | | 21 | D | | 41 | B | | 61 | B | | 81 | B |
| 2 | A | | 22 | A | | 42 | D | | 62 | C | | 82 | C |
| 3 | C | | 23 | A | | 43 | B | | 63 | B | | 83 | B |
| 4 | B | | 24 | B | | 44 | D | | 64 | C | | 84 | D |
| 5 | B | | 25 | D | | 45 | B | | 65 | C | | 85 | B |
| 6 | D | | 26 | C | | 46 | D | | 66 | C | | 86 | D |
| 7 | A | | 27 | D | | 47 | A | | 67 | A | | 87 | B |
| 8 | B | | 28 | A | | 48 | C | | 68 | D | | 88 | A |
| 9 | B | | 29 | A | | 49 | C | | 69 | A | | 89 | C |
| 10 | A | | 30 | B | | 50 | D | | 70 | B | | 90 | C |
| 11 | B | | 31 | C | | 51 | C | | 71 | A | | 91 | D |
| 12 | A | | 32 | C | | 52 | D | | 72 | B | | 92 | A |
| 13 | B | | 33 | A | | 53 | A | | 73 | C | | | |
| 14 | C | | 34 | B | | 54 | C | | 74 | A | | | |
| 15 | A | | 35 | A | | 55 | C | | 75 | B | | | |
| 16 | C | | 36 | C | | 56 | B | | 76 | D | | | |
| 17 | A | | 37 | B | | 57 | C | | 77 | D | | | |
| 18 | A | | 38 | A | | 58 | D | | 78 | A | | | |
| 19 | D | | 39 | D | | 59 | C | | 79 | A | | | |
| 20 | B | | 40 | B | | 60 | B | | 80 | C | | | |

## Crossword Answers – The Cardiovascular System

### Crossword 1

**Across**
1. Erythrocytes
4. Tricuspid
5. High
9. Maxillary
12. Age
13. Plasma
14. Pulse
15. Oxygen

**Down**
2. Endocardium
3. Right Atrium
6. Heart
7. Vein
8. Pulmonary
10. Arteries
11. Gases

### Crossword 2

**Across**
3. Bicuspid
5. Myocardium
8. Hypotension
9. Leucocytes
11. Cephalic
13. Arterioles
14. Cardiac Cycle

**Down**
1. Autonomic
2. Ventricles
4. Platelets
6. Phlebitis
7. Rhesus Factor
10. Valves
12. Aorta

## Crossword 3

**Across**
1. Thrombocytes
4. Exercise
7. Waste
8. Pacemaker
9. Ascending
12. Oxygenated
14. Brachial
15. Capillaries

**Down**
2. Systemic
3. Pericardium
5. Coronary
6. Septicaemia
10. Carotid
11. Systole
13. Albumin

## Crossword 4

**Across**
1. Sphygmomanometer
4. Left Ventricle
7. Blood
10. Prothrombin
11. Pulmonary Artery
14. Carbon Dioxide
15. Femoral
17. Calcium
18. Serous
19. Red
20. Leucocytes

**Down**
2. Haemophilia
3. Antigen
5. Antibodies
6. Blood Pressure
8. Arteriosclerosis
9. Fibrin
12. Anaemia
13. Venous
16. Jugular

## Crossword 5

**Across**
3. Hypertension
4. Low
5. Veins
8. Type AB
9. Deoxygenated
11. Erythrocytes
14. Capillaries
16. Atherosclerosis
17. Vitamin K
18. Squamous
19. Basilic
20. Albumin

**Down**
1. Thrombosis
2. Interstitial
6. Leukaemia
7. Skeletal
10. Oxyhaemoglobin
12. Occipital
13. Septum
15. Liver

# Chapter 6 | The Lymphatic System

## Multiple Choice Questions

| | |
|---|---|
| **1. Which one of the following does lymph not contain?**<br>a) Erythrocytes<br>b) Leucocytes<br>c) Waste materials<br>d) Lymphoctyes<br><br>*Answer:* _____ | **2. What are lymphatic capillaries?**<br>a) Capillaries which transport lymph around the lymphatic system<br>b) Muscular tissue which prevent the back flow of lymph<br>c) Vessels which transport waste materials to the lymph nodes<br>d) Vessels which collect excess tissue fluid and waste products<br><br>*Answer:* _____ |
| **3. What type of valves do lymphatic vessels have?**<br>a) Bicuspid valves<br>b) Semi lunar valves<br>c) Tricuspid valves<br>d) Micuspid valves<br><br>*Answer:* _____ | **4. The inner layer of the lymphatic vessels is made up of;**<br>a) Muscular tissue<br>b) Endothelial cells<br>c) Elastic tissue<br>d) Fibrous tissue<br><br>*Answer:* _____ |
| **5. An efferent lymphatic vessel transports lymph;**<br>a) To the lymphatic ducts<br>b) Back to the system<br>c) To the lymph nodes<br>d) To the lymphatic vessels<br><br>*Answer:* _____ | **6. Which one of the following is not a function of lymph nodes?**<br>a) To collect lymph and convey it to the heart<br>b) To form anitbodies against a particular infection<br>c) To filter lymph<br>d) To produce new lymphocytes and antibodies<br><br>*Answer:* _____ |

| | |
|---|---|
| **7. Which one of the following does lymphatic tissue not contain?**<br>a) Phagocytes<br>b) Lymphoctyes<br>c) Cells dividing to form new lymphoctyes<br>d) Erythrocytes<br><br>*Answer:* _____ | **8. Where is the right lymphatic duct positioned?**<br>a) Chest<br>b) Leg<br>c) Arm<br>d) Neck<br><br>*Answer:* _____ |
| **9. How long is the thoracic duct?**<br>a) 40cm<br>b) 1.5cm<br>c) 10cm<br>d) 2.5cm<br><br><br>*Answer:* _____ | **10. Where are the axillary nodes located?**<br>a) At the back of the skull<br>b) Tonsils<br>c) Armpits<br>d) Legs<br><br>*Answer:* _____ |
| **11. Where is the spleen positioned?**<br>a) Under the diaphragm<br>b) Behind the lungs<br>c) Upper left side of the abdomen<br>d) Upper right side of the abdomen<br><br><br>*Answer:* _____ | **12. Cancer of the lymphatic tissue is called?**<br>a) Hodgkin's disease<br>b) Addison's syndrome<br>c) Cushing's syndrome<br>d) Septicemia<br><br>*Answer:* _____ |
| **13. Obstruction of the lymphatic flow causes;**<br>a) Atherosclerosis<br>b) Oedema<br>c) Blood clotting<br>d) Hodgkin's disease<br><br>*Answer:* _____ | **14. Lymphatic capillaries join up to become;**<br>a) Lymph nodes<br>b) Lymphatic vessels<br>c) Lymphatic tissue<br>d) Lymphatic ducts<br><br>*Answer:* _____ |
| **15. What are lymph nodes made of?**<br>a) Lymphatic tissue<br>b) Fibrous tissue<br>c) Elastic tissue<br>d) Muscular tissue<br><br>*Answer:* _____ | **16. The popliteal nodes are located;**<br>a) In the neck<br>b) Behind the knee<br>c) On the tonsils<br>d) In the spleen<br><br>*Answer:* _____ |

**17. What does the spleen destroy?**

a) Leucocytes
b) Lymphocytes
c) Foreign particles
d) Thrombocytes and erythrocytes

*Answer:* _____

**18. What is the function of lymphatic vessels?**

a) Transport lymph to the spleen
b) Transport lymph to the lymphatic capillaries
c) Transport lymph to the lymphatic ducts
d) Transport lymph towards the heart

*Answer:* _____

**19. Lymphatic tissue contains;**

a) Erythrocytes
b) Thrombocytes
c) Leucocytes
d) Phagocytes

*Answer:* _____

**20. Filtered lymph passes into;**

a) Lymphatic nodes
b) Lymphatic ducts
c) Lymphatic capillaries
d) Lymphatic tissue

*Answer:* _____

**21. The thoracic duct is positioned;**

a) Leg
b) Arm
c) Hand
d) Torso

*Answer:* _____

**22. The submandibular nodes are located;**

a) Face
b) Arms
c) Legs
d) Chest

*Answer:* _____

**23. Which one of the following is not a function of the spleen?**

a) Forms new leucocytes
b) Removes foreign particles
c) Helps fight infection
d) Acts as a blood reservoir

*Answer:* _____

**24. Which one of the following does not help to circulate lymph?**

a) Suction
b) Contraction of skeletal muscles
c) Heat
d) Pressure

*Answer:* _____

**25. Where to lymphatic capillaries not occur?**

a) Central nervous system
b) Autonomic nervous system
c) Peripheral nervous system
d) Cranial nerves

*Answer:* _____

**26. The outer layer of lymphatic vessels consist of;**

a) Muscular tissue
b) Elastic tissue
c) Fibrous tissue
d) Endothelial cells

*Answer:* _____

**27. An afferent vessel carries lymph;**
a) Around the body
b) To the lymph ducts
c) To the lymph nodes
d) To lymph capillaries

*Answer: _____*

**28. Trabecula are;**
a) Inward strands of elastic tissue
b) Inward strands of fibrous tissue
c) Inward strands of lymphatic tissue
d) Inward strands of muscular tissue

*Answer: _____*

**29. How long is the right lymphatic duct?**
a) 1.5cm
b) 4cm
c) 2cm
d) 2.5cm

*Answer: _____*

**30. The occipital nodes are located;**
a) On the face
b) At the back of the skull
c) Armpits
d) Elbows

*Answer: _____*

**31. What is the structure of the spleen?**
a) An inner capsule of fibrous tissue
b) An outer capsule of fibrous tissue
c) An inner capsule of elastic tissue
d) An outer capsule of elastic tissue

*Answer: _____*

**32. What is the function of the right lymphatic duct?**
a) Drains lymph into the head, neck and torso
b) Collects lymph from the right side of the body
c) Collects lymph from the right side of the head and neck, chest and right arm
d) Collects lymph from the left side of the body

*Answer: _____*

**33. Trabeculae are located;**
a) In lymphatic tissue
b) In lymphatic ducts
c) In lymphatic capillaries
d) In lymph nodes

*Answer: _____*

**34. What is the structure of lymphatic vessels?**
a) Thick walled, collapsible vessels carrying lymph
b) Thick walled, collapsible tubules
c) Thin walled, collapsible vessels carrying lymph
d) Thin walled, collapsible vessels

*Answer: _____*

| | |
|---|---|
| **35. Which one of the following is a function of lymph?**<br>a) Carry excess tissue fluid away from tissue space<br>b) Remove and destroy harmful bacteria<br>c) Transports excess waste away from tissues<br>d) Transport oxygen to the lymphatic capillaries<br><br><br>*Answer:* _____ | **36. What is the structure of lymphatic capillaries?**<br>a) Fine blind ended permeable tubes<br>b) Fine blind ended hollow permeable tubes<br>c) Fine blind ended permeable tubes, composed of a single layer of endothelial cells<br>d) Fine blind ended permeable tubes composed of a single layer of epothelial tissue<br><br>*Answer:* _____ |
| **37. What is the middle layer of the lymphatic vessels made up of?**<br>a) Endothelial cells<br>b) Fibrous tissue<br>c) Muscular tissue<br>d) Muscular and elastic tissue<br><br>*Answer:* _____ | **38. Lymphatic vessels open up into;**<br>a) Lymph nodes<br>b) Lymph duct<br>c) Lymph tissue<br>d) Lymph capillaries<br><br><br>*Answer:* _____ |
| **39. Which vein does the right lymphatic duct pass into?**<br>a) Right renal vein<br>b) Right iliac vein<br>c) Right subclavian vein<br>d) Right carotid vein<br><br><br><br><br><br><br>*Answer:* _____ | **40. Which of the following is a function of the thoracic duct?**<br>a) Collects lymph from the left side of the body<br>b) Collects lymph from the left side of the head, neck, lower limbs, left side of the trunk and left arm<br>c) Collects lymph from the left side of the head, neck, left leg, left side of the trunk and left arm<br>d) Collects lymph from the right side of the body<br><br>*Answer:* _____ |

| | |
|---|---|
| **41. The supratrochlear nodes are located;**<br>a) Behind the ears<br>b) Armpits<br>c) Behind the knees<br>d) Elbows<br><br><br><br>*Answer:* _____ | **42. What is the relationship between the lymphatic system and muscular systems?**<br>a) Excess waste and toxins are transported<br>b) Lactic acid is drained away in the lymphatic system<br>c) Fats are absorbed<br>d) Glucose is converted into fat<br><br>*Answer:* _____ |
| **43. What is the function of lymphatic capillaries?**<br>a) To carry excess tissue fluid and waste products away from tissue spaces of the body<br>b) To collect lymph and transport it to the heart<br>c) To transport excess waste<br>d) To transport monocytes and lymphocytes to the blood<br><br>*Answer:* _____ | **44. How many layers do lymphatic vessels have?**<br>a) 3<br>b) 2<br>c) 4<br>d) 1<br><br><br><br><br><br><br>*Answer:* _____ |
| **45. The inguinal nodes are located;**<br>a) Groin area<br>b) Behind the knees<br>c) Elbows<br>d) Armpits<br><br>*Answer:* _____ | **46. What is lymphadenitis?**<br>a) Inflammation of lymphatic capillaries<br>b) Inflammation of lymphatic vessels<br>c) Inflammation of lymphatic tissue<br>d) Inflammation of lymph nodes<br><br>*Answer:* _____ |

# The Lymphatic System - Crossword 1

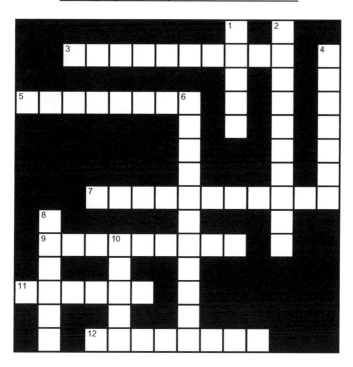

## Across

3. Inward strands of fibrous tissue (10)
5. Lymph node in the groin area (8)
7. White blood cells that produce antibodies (11)
9. Lymph node behind the knee (9)
11. Swelling due to excess fluid in the body tissues (6)
12. Which lymphatic duct drains lymph from the lower limbs? (8)

## Down

1. What does the spleen store? (5)
2. Cells found in lymph (10)
4. What type of tissue is the outer layer of lymphatic vessels made up of? (7)
6. Oedema associated with an obstruction in the lymphatic vessels (11)
8. What organ helps to protect against disease? (6)
10. A fluid found in lymphatic capillaries (5)

# The Lymphatic System - Crossword 2

**Across**

2. What type of cells are found in lymph? (11)
5. White blood cells which destroy bacteria and harmful matter (10)
6. Nodes found in the armpits (8)
8. Valves in lymphatic vessels which ensure that lymph flows in the right direction (9)
9. Which lymphatic duct lies in the root of the neck? (5)
10. Vessel which drains the filtered lymph from the node (8)

**Down**

1. Cancer of the lymphatic tissues (15)
3. Lymph node at the elbow (14)
4. What part of the lymphatic system acts as filters of lymph? (10)
7. Vessels which transport lymph around the lymphatic system (9)

## Multiple Choice Answers – The Lymphatic System

| 1 | A | 21 | D | 41 | D |
|---|---|----|---|----|---|
| 2 | D | 22 | A | 42 | B |
| 3 | B | 23 | A | 43 | A |
| 4 | B | 24 | C | 44 | A |
| 5 | B | 25 | A | 45 | A |
| 6 | A | 26 | C | 46 | D |
| 7 | D | 27 | C | | |
| 8 | D | 28 | B | | |
| 9 | A | 29 | A | | |
| 10 | C | 30 | B | | |
| 11 | C | 31 | B | | |
| 12 | A | 32 | C | | |
| 13 | B | 33 | D | | |
| 14 | B | 34 | C | | |
| 15 | A | 35 | C | | |
| 16 | B | 36 | C | | |
| 17 | D | 37 | D | | |
| 18 | D | 38 | A | | |
| 19 | D | 39 | C | | |
| 20 | B | 40 | B | | |

## Crossword Answers – The Lymphatic System

### Crossword 1

**Across**
3. Trabeculae
5. Inguinal
7. Lymphocytes
9. Popliteal
11. Oedema
12. Thoracic

**Down**
1. Blood
2. Leucocytes
4. Fibrous
6. Lymphoedema
8. Spleen
10. Lymph

### Crossword 2

**Across**
2. Lymphocytes
5. Phagocytes
6. Axillary
8. Semi Lunar
9. Right
10. Efferent

**Down**
1. Hodgkin's Disease
3. Supratrochlear
4. Lymph Nodes
7. Lymphatic

# Chapter 7 | The Endocrine System

## Multiple Choice Questions

| | |
|---|---|
| **1. Hyposecretion can be defined as;**<br>a) Over production of a hormone<br>b) Where 2 or more hormones are produced<br>c) Where only 1 hormone is secreted<br>d) Under production of a hormone<br><br>*Answer:* _____ | **2. What is the function of glucocorticoids?**<br>a) Regulates thyroid gland<br>b) Controls male sex hormones<br>c) Metabolises proteins, carbohydrates and fats<br>d) Regulates basic metabolic rate<br><br>*Answer:* _____ |
| **3. Which one of the following is a function of adrenaline?**<br>a) Constricts blood vessels to raise blood pressure<br>b) Responsible for male sexual characteristics<br>c) Activates vitamin D<br>d) Responsible for female characteristics<br><br>*Answer:* _____ | **4. The condition in which menstruation stops is known as;**<br>a) Addison's syndrome<br>b) Cushing's syndrome<br>c) Amenorrhoea<br>d) Polycystic ovarian syndrome<br><br><br>*Answer:* _____ |
| **5. The thymus is located;**<br>a) Centre of the brain<br>b) In the thorax<br>c) Either side of the neck<br>d) Base of the brain<br><br>*Answer:* _____ | **6. What is the function of insulin and glucagon?**<br>a) Regulates salts in the body<br>b) Maintains calcium levels in the body<br>c) Stabilise blood sugar levels<br>d) Regulates water absorption<br><br>*Answer:* _____ |
| **7. A hormone is a;**<br>a) Chemical catalyst<br>b) Chemical reaction<br>c) Chemical messenger<br>d) Chemical enzyme<br><br>*Answer:* _____ | **8. What hormone regulates the thyroid gland?**<br>a) Parathormone<br>b) Thyroid stimulating hormone<br>c) Luteinising hormone<br>d) Insulin<br><br>*Answer:* _____ |

| | |
|---|---|
| **9. Hyposecretion of antidiuretic hormone causes;**<br>a) Addison's disease<br>b) High blood pressure<br>c) Diabetes insipidus<br>d) Muscular atrophy<br><br>*Answer:* _____ | **10. What is the function of calcitonin?**<br>a) Helps glucose enter cells<br>b) Controls body rhythms<br>c) Controls calcium levels in the blood<br>d) Sexual development<br><br>*Answer:* _____ |
| **11. Hypersecretion of mineralocorticoids causes;**<br>a) Addison's disease<br>b) Muscle atrophy<br>c) High blood pressure<br>d) Cushings syndrome<br><br>*Answer:* _____ | **12. Which hormone does the adrenal medulla secrete?**<br>a) Glucocorticoids<br>b) Adrenaline<br>c) Insulin<br>d) Testosterone<br><br>*Answer:* _____ |
| **13. Where is the pineal gland located?**<br>a) Behind the thyroid gland<br>b) Either side of the neck<br>c) Behind the scrotum<br>d) Centre of the brain<br><br>*Answer:* _____ | **14. Hypersecretion can be defined as;**<br>a) Too much of a hormone is produced<br>b) Not enough of a hormone is produced<br>c) No hormones are produced<br>d) A balance of hormones are produced<br><br>*Answer:* _____ |
| **15. Which hormone controls the adrenal cortex?**<br>a) Adrenaline<br>b) Prolactin<br>c) Adrenocorticotropin<br>d) Thyrotrophin<br><br>*Answer:* _____ | **16. Which stage of the menstrual cycle does ovulation occur?**<br>a) Menstrual cycle<br>b) Secretory phase<br>c) Menopause<br>d) Proliferative phase<br><br>*Answer:* _____ |
| **17. Which one of the following is a function of melatonin?**<br>a) Sexual development<br>b) Stimulates tissue metabolism<br>c) Maintains BMR<br>d) Controls body rhythms<br><br>*Answer:* _____ | **18. An endocrine gland;**<br>a) Is a chemical messenger<br>b) A ductless gland which produces hormones<br>c) A hormone<br>d) A ductless gland<br><br>*Answer:* _____ |

**19. What hormone stimulates growth of the mammary glands and lactation after parturition?**
a) Follicle stimulating hormone
b) Lactogenic hormone
c) Human growth hormone
d) Thyroxin

Answer: _____

**20. Which part of the nervous system does the adrenal medulla support?**
a) Sympathetic nervous system
b) Central nervous system
c) Peripheral nervous system
d) Parasympathetic nervous system

Answer: _____

**21. Which one of the following is a phase of the menstrual cycle?**
a) Menstrual phase
b) Prophase
c) Endometrium phase
d) Amenorrhoea phase

Answer: _____

**22. Hypersecretion of glucocorticoids causes;**
a) Cushing's syndrome
b) Addison's Disease
c) Graves disease
d) Diabetes insipidus

Answer: _____

**23. What is the function of HGH?**
a) Stimulates production of melanin
b) Regulates height and growth
c) Controls body rhythms
d) Produces milk during lactation

Answer: _____

**24. Hypersecretion of testosterone in women causes;**
a) Cushing's syndrome
b) Amenorrhoea
c) Addisons disease
d) Breast growth

Answer: _____

**25. Which hormone is produced by the pineal gland?**
a) Glucogen
b) Melatonin
c) Adrenaline
d) Parathormone

Answer: _____

**26. Where are the pituitary glands located?**
a) Base of the brain
b) Either side of the neck
c) Either side of the uterus
d) On top of the kidneys

Answer: _____

**27. Hyposecretion of thyroxine causes;**
a) Cretinism
b) Amenorrhoea
c) Sweating
d) Fatigue

Answer: _____

**28. Which of the following is a function of oxytocin?**
a) Ovulation
b) Hair growth
c) Regulates blood sugar levels
d) Contracts uterus during childbirth

Answer: _____

| | |
|---|---|
| **29. Where are the ovaries located?**<br>a) Either side of the uterus<br>b) Above the uterus<br>c) Below the uterus<br>d) Between duodenum and spleen<br><br><br>*Answer:* _____ | **30. What endocrine gland is located in the centre of the brain?**<br>a) Pituitary<br>b) Pineal body<br>c) Pancreas<br>d) Parathyroid<br><br><br>*Answer:* _____ |
| **31. Insulin is secreted by;**<br>a) Pancreas<br>b) Adrenal cortex<br>c) Pineal gland<br>d) Thyroid glands<br><br><br><br>*Answer:* _____ | **32. Which one of the following is not a function of follicle stimulating hormone?**<br>a) Production of progesterone<br>b) Stimulates ovaries to produce oestrogen<br>c) Stimulates testes to produce sperm<br>d) Ovulation in women<br><br>*Answer:* _____ |
| **33. Hyposecretion of HGH causes;**<br>a) Oedema<br>b) High blood pressure<br>c) Kidney failure<br>d) Dwarfism<br><br><br>*Answer:* _____ | **34. Which hormone is responsible for sexual development?**<br>a) Testes<br>b) Ovaries<br>c) Luteinising hormone<br>d) Gonadotrophins<br><br><br>*Answer:* _____ |
| **35. Hypersecretion of parathormone causes;**<br>a) Spasms in hands and feet<br>b) Kidney failure<br>c) Addison's syndrome<br>d) Brittle bones<br><br>*Answer:* _____ | **36. Where is the pancreas located?**<br>a) Above the stomach<br>b) In the abdomen, partially behind the stomach<br>c) Behind the lungs<br>d) In between the lungs<br><br>*Answer:* _____ |
| **37. Approximately how long does the menstrual cycle last?**<br>a) 7 days<br>b) 32 days<br>c) 28 days<br>d) 14 days<br><br><br>*Answer:* _____ | **38. What is the function of melanocyte stimulating hormone?**<br>a) Stimulates the release of melanin<br>b) Controls the activity of the thyroid gland<br>c) Controls sexual development<br>d) Regulates salts in the body<br><br>*Answer:* _____ |

**39. Hypersecretion of thyroxin causes;**

a) Addison's disease

b) Grave's disease

c) Goitre

d) Convulsions

*Answer:* _____

**40. Where are the parathyroid glands situated?**

a) Either side of the neck

b) On each kidney

c) Base of the brain

d) Behind the thyroid gland

*Answer:* _____

**41. What is the function of mineralocorticoids?**

a) Controls body rhythms

b) Regulates salt levels in the body

c) Maintains calcium levels in blood

d) Controls production of melanin

*Answer:* _____

**42. Hypersecretion of insulin and glucagon causes;**

a) Diabetes mellitus

b) Depression

c) Hypoglycaemia

d) Diabetes insipidus

*Answer:* _____

**43. What gland secretes calcitonin?**

a) Adrenal medulla

b) Pituitary

c) Pancreas

d) Thyroid

*Answer:* _____

**44. What hormone is not produced by the anterior lobe of the pituitary gland?**

a) TSH

b) ACTH

c) Calcitonin

d) Gonadotrophins

*Answer:* _____

**45. What is the function of luteinising hormone?**

a) Stimulates ovaries to produce oestrogen

b) Produces milk during breast feeding

c) Stimulates ovaries to release the egg

d) Produce oestrogen

*Answer:* _____

**46. Where are the thyroid glands located?**

a) Behind the stomach

b) In the neck

c) In the thorax

d) Centre of the brain

*Answer:* _____

**47. Hypersecretion of oestrogen in men causes;**

a) Addison's disease

b) Hair growth

c) Kidney failure

d) Gynaecomastia

*Answer:* _____

**48. A malfunction of melatonin includes;**

a) Fatigue

b) Depression

c) High blood pressure

d) Muscle atrophy

*Answer:* _____

**49. The start of menstruation is known as;**
a) Menopause
b) Menarche
c) Proliferative
d) Menstrual cycle

*Answer:* _____

**50. Which of the following is a function of interstitial cell stimulating hormone?**
a) Maintains BMR
b) Regulates water absorption in kidneys
c) Stimulate testosterone production in males
d) Regulates salts in the body

*Answer:* _____

**51. Hypersecretion of ADH causes;**
a) Oedema
b) Grave's disease
c) Diabetes insipidus
d) Cretinism

*Answer:* _____

**52. What gland produces mineralocorticoids?**
a) Adrenal cortex
b) Thyroid
c) Adrenal medulla
d) Pituitary

*Answer:* _____

**53. Which one of the following is not an effect of Cushing's syndrome?**
a) Weight gain
b) Low blood pressure
c) Muscle weakness
d) Mental illness

*Answer:* _____

**54. Which hormone is produced by the posterior lobe hormones?**
a) TSH
b) HGH
c) ACTH
d) ADH

*Answer:* _____

**55. Which one of the following is a function of the hormones produced by the thyroid glands?**
a) Regulates metabolism
b) Regulates blood sugar levels
c) Produces vitamin D
d) Regulates salt levels

*Answer:* _____

**56. Which glands are situated on top of each kidney?**
a) Thyroid glands
b) Pituitary glands
c) Parathyroids
d) Adrenal glands

*Answer:* _____

**57. Which one of the following is not a function of parathormone?**
a) To prepare the body for fight or flight
b) Regulates calcium levels in blood
c) Vitamin D synthesis
d) Stimulates reabsorption in kidneys

*Answer:* _____

**58. Which hormone is not produced by the adrenal cortex?**
a) Adrenaline
b) Glucocorticoids
c) Mineralocorticoids
d) Sex hormones

*Answer:* _____

| | |
|---|---|
| **59. Hyposecretion of insulin causes;**<br>a) Hypoglycaemia<br>b) Diabetes insipidus<br>c) Sweating<br>d) Diabetes mellitus<br><br>*Answer:* _____ | **60. Where are T Cells found?**<br>a) Pituitary gland<br>b) Thyroid gland<br>c) Thymus<br>d) Adrenal medulla<br><br>*Answer:* _____ |
| **61. What is the function of antidiuretic hormone?**<br>a) Stimulates basic metabolic rate<br>b) Increases water reabsorption in kidneys<br>c) Maintains calcium levels in bones<br>d) Contracts the uterus during labour<br><br>*Answer:* _____ | **62. Which of the following hormones are not produced by the thyroid glands?**<br>a) Thyroxine<br>b) Calcitonin<br>c) Oxytocin<br>d) Triodothyronine<br><br>*Answer:* _____ |
| **63. Which hormone is produced by the parathyroids?**<br>a) Noradrenaline<br>b) Mineralocorticoids<br>c) Parathormone<br>d) Thyroxine<br><br>*Answer:* _____ | **64. Hyposecretion of parathormone causes;**<br>a) Cushing's syndrome<br>b) Tetany<br>c) Low blood sugar levels<br>d) Diabetes insipidus<br><br>*Answer:* _____ |
| **65. What hormone stimulates testosterone production in men?**<br>a) Interstitial cell stimulating hormone<br>b) Follicle stimulating hormone<br>c) Lactogenic hormone<br>d) Adrenocorticotrophin<br><br>*Answer:* _____ | |

## The Endocrine System - Crossword 1

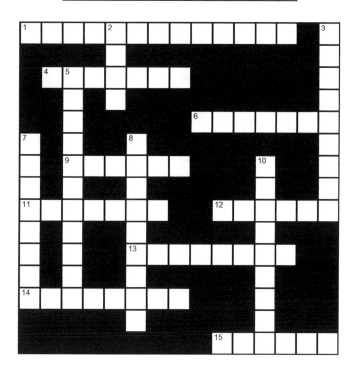

**Across**

1. An adrenal gland (13)
4. What is calcitonin responsible for controlling in the blood? (7)
6. A chemical messenger (7)
9. What does the hypersecretion of antidiuretic hormone cause? (6)
11. Gland found on the kidneys (7)
12. What does the hyposecretion of parathormone cause? (6)
13. Posterior lobe hormone (8)
14. What does the hyposecretion of HGH cause? (8)
15. Gland found in the thorax (6)

**Down**

2. Where are the thyroid glands found? (4)
3. A phase of the menstrual cycle (9)
5. Absence of menstruation (11)
7. What does parathormone activate? (8)
8. What is the pineal body responsible for the production of? (9)
10. Gland situated at the base of the brain (9)

# The Endocrine System - Crossword 2

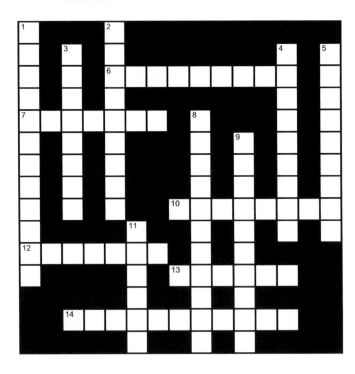

## Across

6. A ductless gland (9)
7. Progesterone is a hormone secreted by which gland? (7)
10. Glucagon is a hormone produced by which endocrine gland? (8)
12. Hormone of the pancreas (7)
13. What phase is the proliferative phase of the menstrual cycle? (6)
14. Polycystic ovarian syndrome is caused by the hyposecretion of which hormone? (11)

## Down

1. What hormone controls the thyroid gland? (12)
2. What does the hyposecretion of thyroxin in childhood cause? (9)
3. Start of menstruation (8)
4. Hormone secreted by the ovaries (9)
5. A condition which causes menstruation to stop (9)
8. What part of the nervous system controls hormones secreted by the adrenal medulla? (11)
9. Hormone secreted by the thyroid glands (10)
11. Organ where the adrenal glands are located (6)

# The Endocrine System – Crossword 3

**Across**

1. A hormone produced by the thyroid gland (12)
5. Glands which produce testosterone (6)
9. A hormone which stimulates the ovaries to produce oestrogen (19)
13. What hormone regulates carbohydrate, fat and protein metabolism? (15)
16. What hormone causes the breathing and pulse rate to increase? (10)
17. What gland is found in the neck? (7)
18. Tissue that looks and acts like the lining of the uterus, that grows outside the uterus (13)
19. What condition is caused by the hyposecretion of insulin? (16)
20. What can the hypersecretion of insulin lead to? (13)

**Down**

2. What hormone regulates the development of the male secondary sex characteristics in puberty? (12)

3. What hormone controls the growth of muscles and long bones? (11)

4. What does the hypersecretion of glucocorticoids cause? (16)

6. A hormone released when a person is in the dark, resulting in them becoming sleepy? (9)

7. What hormone is released to restore blood sugar levels when they are too low? (8)

8. What does the hypersecretion of growth hormone cause? (9)

10. First phase of the menstrual cycle (9)

11. What do glucocorticoids metabolise? (8)

12. A lobe of the pituitary gland (9)

14. What part of the endocrine system releases hormones? (5)

15.  A salt which the hormones of the adrenal cortex help to regulate (9)

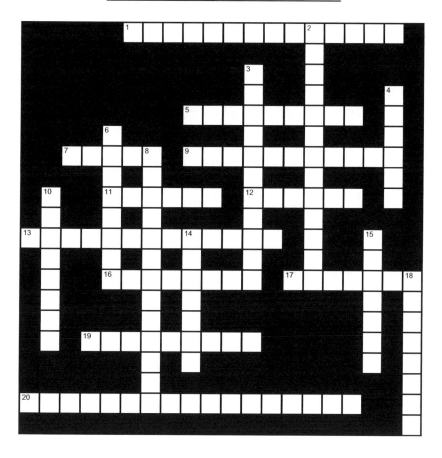

**Across**

1. What hormone controls the development of the ovaries and testes? (14)
5. A hormone secreted by the thymus (9)
7. Where is the pituitary gland located? (5)
9. Antidiuretic hormone (11)
11. Which adrenal gland secretes mineralocorticoids? (6)
12. What is caused by a deficiency of calcium in the blood? (6)
13. What does the hypersecretion of thyroxine cause? (13)
16. What are some hormones made of? (8)
17. Which adrenal gland is under the control of the sympathetic nervous system? (7)
19. What hormone is responsible for milk production milk from the breasts following birth? (9)
20. What does the hyposecretion of ADH cause? (17)

**Down**

2. Second phase of the menstrual cycle (13)
3. What do the endocrine and nervous systems work together to achieve? (11)
4. What organ are the adrenal glands situated on top of? (6)
6. Where are the islets of langerhans located? (8)
8. A hormone secreted by the adrenal medulla (13)
10. What can the hypersecretion of testosterone in females lead to? (8)
14. What organ is the pancreas located behind? (7)
15. What does the hormone MSH produce? (7)
18. Which lobe of the pituitary gland secretes TSH? (8)

## Multiple Choice Answers – The Endocrine System

| # | | | # | | | # | | | # | |
|----|---|---|----|---|---|----|---|---|----|---|
| 1 | D | | 21 | A | | 41 | B | | 61 | B |
| 2 | C | | 22 | A | | 42 | C | | 62 | C |
| 3 | A | | 23 | B | | 43 | D | | 63 | C |
| 4 | C | | 24 | B | | 44 | C | | 64 | B |
| 5 | B | | 25 | B | | 45 | C | | 65 | A |
| 6 | C | | 26 | A | | 46 | B | | | |
| 7 | C | | 27 | A | | 47 | D | | | |
| 8 | B | | 28 | D | | 48 | B | | | |
| 9 | C | | 29 | A | | 49 | B | | | |
| 10 | C | | 30 | B | | 50 | C | | | |
| 11 | C | | 31 | A | | 51 | A | | | |
| 12 | B | | 32 | A | | 52 | A | | | |
| 13 | D | | 33 | D | | 53 | B | | | |
| 14 | A | | 34 | D | | 54 | D | | | |
| 15 | C | | 35 | D | | 55 | A | | | |
| 16 | D | | 36 | B | | 56 | D | | | |
| 17 | D | | 37 | C | | 57 | A | | | |
| 18 | B | | 38 | A | | 58 | A | | | |
| 19 | B | | 39 | B | | 59 | D | | | |
| 20 | A | | 40 | D | | 60 | C | | | |

## Crossword Answers – The Endocrine System

### Crossword 1

**Across**
1. Adrenal Cortex
4. Calcium
6. Hormone
9. Oedema
11. Adrenal
12. Tetany
13. Oxytocin
14. Dwarfism
15. Thymus

**Down**
2. Neck
3. Secretory
5. Amenorrhoea
7. Vitamin D
8. Melatonin
10. Pituitary

### Crossword 2

**Across**
6. Endocrine
7. Ovaries
10. Pancreas
12. Insulin
13. Second
14. Luteinising

**Down**
1. Thyrotrophin
2. Cretinism
3. Menarche
4. Oestrogen
5. Menopause
8. Sympathetic
9. Calcitonin
11. Kidney

## Crossword 3

**Across**

1. Thymic Factor
5. Testes
9. Follicle Stimulating
13. Glucocorticoids
16. Adrenaline
17. Thyroid
18. Endometriosis
19. Diabetes Mellitus
20. Hypoglycaemia

**Down**

2. Testosterone
3. Human Growth
4. Cushing's Syndrome
6. Melatonin
7. Glucagon
8. Gigantism
10. Menstrual
11. Proteins
12. Posterior
14. Gland
15. Potassium

## Crossword 4

**Across**

1. Gonadotrophins
5. Thymosine
7. Brain
9. Vasopressin
11. Cortex
12. Tetany
13. Grave's Disease
16. Steroids
17. Medulla
19. Prolactin
20. Diabetes Insipidus

**Down**

2. Proliferative
3. Homeostasis
4. Kidney
6. Pancreas
8. Noradrenaline
10. Virilism
14. Stomach
15. Melanin
18. Anterior

# Chapter 8 | The Nervous System

## Multiple Choice Questions

| | |
|---|---|
| **1. What is the function of neuroglia?**<br>a) Transmit stimuli to the cell body<br>b) Supports the neurones<br>c) Transmit stimuli away from the cell body<br>d) Insulates the axon<br><br>*Answer:* _____ | **2. Which one of the following is not a function of the cerebrum?**<br>a) Controls thought and memory<br>b) Controls feelings of pain<br>c) Controls muscle tone and posture<br>d) Controls conscious movement<br><br>*Answer:* _____ |
| **3. The reflex arc consists of;**<br>a) A sensory organ, the spinal cord, sensory neurons, motor neurons<br>b) The spinal cord and brain<br>c) A sensory nerve and organ<br>d) Brain, sense organ, the spinal cord<br><br>*Answer:* _____ | **4. How many pairs of cranial nerves are there?**<br>a) 8<br>b) 12<br>c) 5<br>d) 31<br><br>*Answer:* _____ |
| **5. Which of the following is not one of the main sections of the brain?**<br>a) The cervical plexus<br>b) The brain stem<br>c) The cerebrum<br>d) The cerebellum<br><br>*Answer:* _____ | **6. Where are neurilemma found?**<br>a) Around the axons of peripheral nerves<br>b) Spinal cord<br>c) Brain<br>d) Autonomic nervous system<br><br><br>*Answer:* _____ |
| **7. Which one of the following is a function of the sympathetic nervous system?**<br>a) Constricts blood flow to the heart<br>b) Causes dilation of skeletal blood vessels<br>c) Slows down the heart rate<br>d) Releases acetylcholine<br><br>*Answer:* _____ | **8. Which part of the brain regulates the actions of the heart and lungs?**<br>a) Midbrain<br>b) Hypothalamus<br>c) Pons varolii<br>d) Medulla oblongata<br><br><br>*Answer:* _____ |

**9. Cerebrospinal fluid contains;**

a) Proteins

b) Plasma and proteins

c) Nutrients, salts and proteins

d) Protein and glucose

*Answer:* _____

**10. What does grey matter help with?**

a) Homeostasis

b) Eating

c) Muscle control

d) Sleeping

*Answer:* _____

**11. Neuroglia is a type of;**

a) Nervous tissue

b) Muscular tissue

c) Connective tissue

d) Yellow elastic tissue

*Answer:* _____

**12. Cerebral palsy occurs;**

a) When the brain is damaged during birth

b) From damage to the spinal cord

c) From the degeneration of neurilemma

d) Injury or damage to nerve tissue

*Answer:* _____

**13. The bundle of nerves known as the cauda equina are made up of what part of the spinal nerves?**

a) Lumbar, sacral and coccygeal nerves

b) Cervical, thoracic and lumbar nerves

c) Thoracic, lumbar and sacral nerves

d) Cervical, lumbar and coccygeal nerves

*Answer:* _____

**14. Which one of the following is a function of the cerebrum?**

a) Maintaining homeostasis

b) Controlling conscious movement

c) Carry messages to the spinal cord

d) Carry messages to and from the brain

*Answer:* _____

**15. What is the centre of the nerve cell?**

a) Synapse

b) Axon

c) Cell body

d) Neurilemma

*Answer:* _____

**16. What is the largest part of the brain?**

a) The cerebellum

b) The hypothalamus

c) The brain stem

d) The cerebrum

*Answer:* _____

**17. A reflex is produced by;**

a) Nerve cells

b) Stimulus

c) Nerve endings

d) Voluntary movement

*Answer:* _____

**18. Which system of the body helps the nervous system to maintain homeostasis?**

a) Respiratory system

b) Endocrine system

c) Muscular system

d) Circulatory system

*Answer:* _____

| | |
|---|---|
| **19. The hamstrings are supplied by the;** <br> a) The lumbar plexus <br> b) The sacral plexus <br> c) The brachial plexus <br> d) The coccygeal plexus <br><br> *Answer:* _____ | **20. Grey matter is made up of;** <br> a) Nerve fibres and dendrites <br> b) Nerve fibres and axons <br> c) Neural cell bodies, unmyelinated axons and dendrites <br> d) Neural cell bodies, neurilemma and dendrites <br><br> *Answer:* _____ |
| **21. Which one of the following is a function of the midbrain?** <br> a) Produces reflexes <br> b) Eye movement <br> c) Homeostasis <br> d) Motor control <br><br> *Answer:* _____ | **22. The coccygeal plexus is located;** <br> a) Front of the pelvic cavity <br> b) Right side of the pelvic cavity <br> c) Left side of the pelvic cavity <br> d) Back of the pelvic cavity <br><br> *Answer:* _____ |
| **23. What is the function of neurilemma?** <br> a) To speed up the transport of nerve impulses along the nerve fibre <br> b) Transport nerve impulses away from the cell body <br> c) They pass on the nerve impulse to the dendrites of the next neurone <br> d) The regeneration of peripheral nerve cells <br><br> *Answer:* _____ | **24. What is the smallest region of the brain?** <br> a) Midbrain <br> b) Grey matter <br> c) Parietal lobe <br> d) Cerebral cortex <br><br><br><br> *Answer:* _____ |
| **25. Which one of the following is not a function of cerebrospinal fluid?** <br> a) Forms a cushion between the brain & cranial bones, protecting brain & spinal cord <br> b) Removes metabolic waste and toxins <br> c) Regulates body temperature <br> d) Protects the brain tissue from injury <br><br> *Answer:* _____ | **26. The olfactory nerve describes;** <br> a) Nerve of sight <br> b) Nerve of smell <br> c) Never of touch <br> d) Sensory nerve <br><br><br><br><br><br> *Answer:* _____ |

| | |
|---|---|
| **27. A loss of dopamine occurs when an individual is suffering from;**<br>a) Multiple sclerosis<br>b) Parkinson's disease<br>c) Cerebral palsy<br>d) Myalgic encephalomyelitis<br><br>*Answer:* _____ | **28. The peripheral nervous system contains;**<br>a) Brain<br>b) Spinal cord<br>c) Autonomic nervous system<br>d) Muscle fibres<br><br>*Answer:* _____ |
| **29. Dendrites are;**<br>a) Nerve fibres<br>b) Nerve cells<br>c) Nerve impulses<br>d) Neurones<br><br>*Answer:* _____ | **30. White matter is made of?**<br>a) Bundles of cell bodies<br>b) Bundles of mixed fibres and dendrites<br>c) Bundles of unmyelinated nerve fibres<br>d) Bundles of myelinated nerve fibres<br><br>*Answer:* _____ |
| **31. The outer layer of the meninges is called;**<br>a) Dura mater<br>b) Cerebrospinal fluid<br>c) Arachnoid fluid<br>d) Pia mater<br><br>*Answer:* _____ | **32. Which part of the brain helps with the regulation of metabolism?**<br>a) Hypothalamus<br>b) Cerebrum<br>c) Midbrain<br>d) Cerebellum<br><br>*Answer:* _____ |
| **33. The groin is supplied by;**<br>a) Lumbar plexus<br>b) Coccygeal plexus<br>c) Brachial plexus<br>d) Cervical plexus<br><br><br><br><br><br>*Answer:* _____ | **34. What disease of the nervous system causes the nerve cells in the brain and spinal cord to lose communication with each other?**<br>a) Hodgkin's Disease<br>b) Neuritis<br>c) Parkinson's Disease<br>d) Multiple Sclerosis<br><br>*Answer:* _____ |
| **35. Which one of the following is a function of the Parasympathetic nervous system?**<br>a) Increases the supply of blood<br>b) Slows the heart rate down<br>c) Increases blood circulation<br>d) Increases inspiration<br><br>*Answer:* _____ | **36. Which part of the brain is the relay station?**<br>a) The cerebrum<br>b) The medulla oblongata<br>c) The midbrain<br>d) The pons varolii<br><br><br>*Answer:* _____ |

| | |
|---|---|
| **37. Efferent nerves only transmit to which type of tissue?**<br>a) Muscular tissue<br>b) Elastic tissue<br>c) Muscular and glandular tissue<br>d) Connective tissue<br><br><br>*Answer:* _____ | **38. The function of the axon is to;**<br>a) Carry nerve impulses away from the cell body<br>b) Carry cell bodies away from the nerve impulses<br>c) Carry nerve impulses to the cell body<br>d) Carry nerve impulses away from the neurone<br><br>*Answer:* _____ |
| **39. What type of cells is the nervous system made up of?**<br>a) Osteoblasts<br>b) Neurons<br>c) Catalysts<br>d) Histiocytes<br><br>*Answer:* _____ | **40. The central nervous system consists of;**<br>a) All of the body's internal organs<br>b) Brain<br>c) Cranial and spinal nerves<br>d) Brain and spinal cord<br><br>*Answer:* _____ |
| **41. What is the function of the spinal cord?**<br>a) Carries motor nerve fibres to the autonomic nervous system<br>b) Carries motor and sensory nerve fibres to the peripheral nervous system<br>c) Transmits messages to the brain<br>d) Transmission of nerve signals between the brain and body<br><br>*Answer:* _____ | **42. Where is the sciatic nerve located?**<br>a) Coccygeal plexus<br>b) Lumbar plexus<br>c) Sacral plexus<br>d) Thoracic plexus<br><br><br><br><br><br><br><br>*Answer:* _____ |
| **43. Parkinson's disease is caused by;**<br>a) Damage to nerve endings<br>b) Damage to the myelin sheath<br>c) Damage to basal ganglia of the brain<br>d) Damage to the facial nerve<br><br><br>*Answer:* _____ | **44. Which of the following is not a function of the myelin sheath?**<br>a) Pass on the nerve impulse to the dendrites<br>b) Insulates the axon<br>c) Accelerates the conduction of nerves<br>d) Protects the axon from pressure<br><br>*Answer:* _____ |

| | |
|---|---|
| **45. Which part of the brain controls the balance of the body?**<br>a) The brain stem<br>b) The pons varolli<br>c) The cerebrum<br>d) The cerebellum<br><br>Answer: _____ | **46. How many pairs of spinal nerves does the spinal cord have?**<br>a) 13<br>b) 12<br>c) 31<br>d) 21<br><br>Answer: _____ |
| **47. The function of the phrenic nerve?**<br>a) To send nerve impulses to the diaphragm causing it to contract<br>b) To send nerve impulses to the lungs causing them to contract<br>c) To receive nerve impulses<br>d) To send nerve impulses to and from the brain<br><br>Answer: _____ | **48. Ganglia is another term for;**<br>a) A collection of nerve endings<br>b) Nerve tissue<br>c) A collection of neurones<br>d) A collection of reflexes<br><br>Answer: _____ |
| **49. Chronic fatigue syndrome is also known as;**<br>a) Myalgic encephalomyelitis<br>b) Multiple sclerosis<br>c) Motor neuron disease<br>d) Neuralgia<br><br>Answer: _____ | **50. Cerebrospinal fluid;**<br>a) Is a clear liquid inside and around the brain<br>b) Is a yellow fluid situated in the lining of the brain<br>c) Is a double layer of tough fibrous membrane<br>d) Is a thin vascular membrane<br><br>Answer: _____ |
| **51. What surrounds the axon?**<br>a) Grey matter<br>b) Nodes of ranvier<br>c) Synapse<br>d) Neurilemma<br><br>Answer: _____ | **52. Which one of the following group of nerves is not present in spinal nerves?**<br>a) Cervical<br>b) Thoracic<br>c) Sacral<br>d) Cranial<br><br>Answer: _____ |

**53. The brain stem is made up of 3 parts;**

a) Hypothalamus, midbrain, medulla oblongata

b) Midbrain, pons varolii, medulla oblongata

c) Hypothalamus, pons varolii, medulla oblongata

d) Midbrain, pons varolii, hypothalamus

*Answer:* _____

**54. Which part of the meninges supplies blood to the brain and spinal cord?**

a) Dura mater

b) Outer membrane

c) Pia mater

d) Arachnoid mater

*Answer:* _____

**55. The first 4 cervical nerves are contained within;**

a) Brachial plexus

b) Cervical plexus

c) Lumbar plexus

d) Sacral plexus

*Answer:* _____

**56. Bell's palsy causes;**

a) Facial paralysis

b) Muscular weakness

c) Inflammation of a nerve

d) Loss of muscular coordination

*Answer:* _____

**57. Multiple sclerosis is caused by;**

a) Damage of the myelin sheath from the nerve fibres in the brain

b) Damage of ganglia from nerve tissue

c) Damage of the myelin sheath around the neurons in the brain and spinal cord

d) Damage or injury

*Answer:* _____

**58. What covers the axon?**

a) Neurilemma

b) Synapse

c) Myelin sheath

d) Dendrites

*Answer:* _____

**59. What is the function of end feet?**

a) They pass on the axon impulse to the dendrites of the next neurone

b) They fill a gap between one neurone and the next

c) They help regenerate nerve cells

d) They transmit nerve impulses

*Answer:* _____

**60. Which part of the brain is known as the small brain?**

a) Hypothalamus

b) Cerebellum

c) Cerebrum

d) Midbrain

*Answer:* _____

| | |
|---|---|
| **61. What is the function of the meninges?**<br><br>a) Transports nutrients<br>b) Removes waste products<br>c) Protects the central nervous system<br>d) Keeps pressure around the brain constant<br><br>*Answer:* _____ | **62. The cervical plexus supplies;**<br><br>a) Muscles of the neck<br>b) Muscles from the base of the neck to the fingertips<br>c) Muscles of the lower limbs<br>d) Muscles of the head, neck, top of shoulders and skin<br><br>*Answer:* _____ |
| **63. Which one of the following is not a function of the parasympathetic nervous system?**<br><br>a) Constricts blood flow to the heart muscles<br>b) Slows down the heart rate<br>c) Decreases secretion of digestive juices<br>d) Increased peristalsis<br><br>*Answer:* _____ | **64. A long slender nerve fibre is known as;**<br><br>a) Synapse<br>b) Cell body<br>c) Myelin sheath<br>d) Axon<br><br><br><br>*Answer:* _____ |
| **65. What part of the nerve cell increases the rate at which nerve impulses travel along the fibre?**<br>a) Myelin sheath<br>b) Nodes of ranvier<br>c) End feet<br>d) Dendrites<br><br>*Answer:* _____ | **66. Which one of the following is not a function of the cerebellum?**<br>a) Controls hunger and sleep patterns<br>b) Controls balance of the body<br>c) Controls muscle tone and posture<br>d) Coordinates skeletal muscles<br><br><br>*Answer:* _____ |
| **67. Which part of the brain is responsible for emotions?**<br>a) Medulla oblongata<br>b) Hypothalamus<br>c) Midbrain<br>d) Pons varolii<br><br>*Answer:* _____ | **68. What is the function of the dendrites?**<br>a) A chemical messenger<br>b) Insulation<br>c) Carry impulses away from the cell body<br>d) Carry impulses towards the cell body<br><br>*Answer:* _____ |

| | |
|---|---|
| **69. The gap where one neurone meets another neurone is called;**<br>a) Synapse<br>b) Neurilemma<br>c) Axon<br>d) Nodes of ranvier<br><br>*Answer:* _____ | **70. Which of the following is not part of the medulla oblongata?**<br>a) Cardiac centre<br>b) Nerve centre<br>c) Vasomotor centre<br>d) Reflex centre<br><br>*Answer:* _____ |
| **71. Which part of the body do the thoracic nerves supply?**<br>a) Thighs<br>b) Chest<br>c) Fingertips<br>d) Neck<br><br><br><br><br>*Answer:* _____ | **72. Which one of the following is not a function of the sympathetic nervous system?**<br>a) Slows heart rate<br>b) Releases noradrenaline preparing the body for fight or flight<br>c) Increases inspiration<br>d) Increases blood supply to the heart<br><br>*Answer:* _____ |
| **73. What causes sciatica?**<br>a) Slowness with voluntary movement<br>b) Damage to the nerve tissue<br>c) Injury to the nerve cell<br>d) Degenerated intervertebral discs<br><br>*Answer:* _____ | **74. Neuritis is described as;**<br>a) Facial paralysis<br>b) Inflammation of a thoracic nerve<br>c) Inflammation of a nerve<br>d) Damage to the basal ganglia<br><br>*Answer:* _____ |
| **75. The function of motor nerves is to;**<br>a) Carry nerve impulses from the central nervous system to the muscles, triggering movement<br>b) Carry impulses from all parts of the body to the brain<br>c) Carry nerve fibres from the brain to the muscles, producing movement<br>d) Carry nerve fibres from all parts of the body to the brain<br><br>*Answer:* _____ | **76. Which one of the following is not a function of the hypothalamus?**<br>a) Regulation of the pituitary gland<br>b) Controls body temperature<br>c) Regulation of hunger and thirst<br>d) Secretion of melatonin<br><br><br><br><br>*Answer:* _____ |

| 77. What muscle type does the autonomic nervous system control?<br>a) Striated and involuntary<br>b) Cardiac and skeletal<br>c) Skeletal and smooth<br>d) Smooth and cardiac<br><br>*Answer:* _____ | 78. An attack of pain along a nerve is known as;<br>a) Parkinson's disease<br>b) Neuralgia<br>c) Neuritis<br>d) Motor neurone disease<br><br>*Answer:* _____ |
|---|---|
| **79. Motor nerves are also known as;**<br>a) Afferent nerves<br>b) Grey matter<br>c) Sensory nerves<br>d) Efferent nerves<br><br>*Answer:* _____ | **80. Cerebal palsy affects;**<br>a) Sensory organs<br>b) Nerve endings<br>c) Nerve fibres<br>d) Movement and posture<br><br>*Answer:* _____ |
| **81. A mini stroke is known as;**<br>a) Transient ischaemic attack<br>b) Myasthenia gravis<br>c) Poliomyelitis<br>d) Peripheral neuropathy<br><br>*Answer:* _____ | |

# The Nervous System - Crossword 1

## Across

3. Part of the brain which transmits messages to and from the spinal cord (11)
7. A nerve fibre which transmits nerve impulses away from the cell body (4)
8. The relay station of the brain (8)
12. Nervous system of the brain and spinal cord (7)
13. Afferent neurones (7)
14. Nerve which sends nerve impulses to the diaphragm telling it to contract (7)
15. Connective tissue which protects the central nervous system (8)

## Down

1. The voluntary part of the peripheral nervous system (7)
2. Plexus which supplies muscles and skin of the shoulder and arm (8)
4. Four cavities inside the brain (10)
5. Branch of the trigeminal nerve which supplies the lower eyelid, upper gums and lip, cheek, teeth and nose (9)
6. Small brain (10)
9. Part of the brain controlling voluntary movements (8)
10. Inflammation of a nerve (8)
11. The gap where one neurone meets another (7)

## The Nervous System - Crossword 2

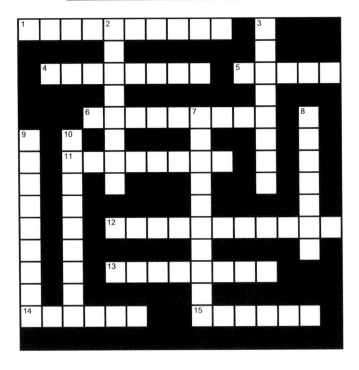

**Across**

1. Facial paralysis (10)
4. The largest section of the brain (8)
5. Neurones which carry impulses from the brain and spinal cord to muscles and glands (5)
6. A connective tissue which supports and protects the neurones (9)
11. Layer of the meninges (8)
12. Which part of the nervous system prepares the body in times of stress or emergencies? (11)
13. Pain down the lower back, thigh, leg and foot (8)
14. Plexus which supplies the muscle and skin of the pelvis (6)
15. A quick automatic movement caused by a sensory stimulus (6)

**Down**

2. What type of muscle does the somatic nervous system control? (8)
3. Plexus which supplies the chest muscles (8)
7. What is the surface layer of the cerebrum made of? (10)
8. Groups of nerve fibres (7)
9. Nerve fibres which carry nerve impulses towards the cell body (9)
10. Branch of the trigeminal nerve which supplies the upper eyelids, eyebrows and forehead (9)

# The Nervous System - Crossword 3

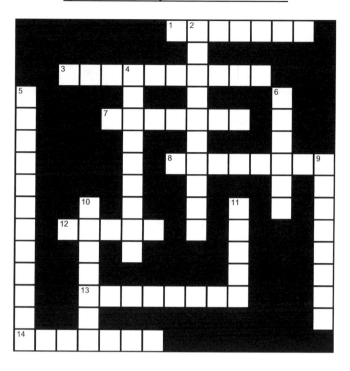

## Across

1. Ends of Axon terminals (7)
3. A branch of the trigeminal nerve which supplies the lower teeth and gums (10)
7. Part of the 11th accessory cranial nerves (7)
8. Nerve cells (8)
12. Nerves which consist of both motor and sensory nerve fibres (5)
13. Secreted by the hypothalamus (8)
14. Nerves which transmit impulses from sensory organs to the brain and spinal cord (7)

## Down

2. A fine delicate membrane only found in the peripheral nerves (10)
4. Layer of the meninges (9)
5. Part of the brain that controls hunger and sleep patterns (12)
6. 31 pairs of these nerves are found in the nervous system (6)
9. The cervical plexus supplies which part of the body? (8)
10. What type of membrane is the dura mater made up of? (7)
11. The organ that fills the cranium (5)

## The Nervous System – Crossword 4

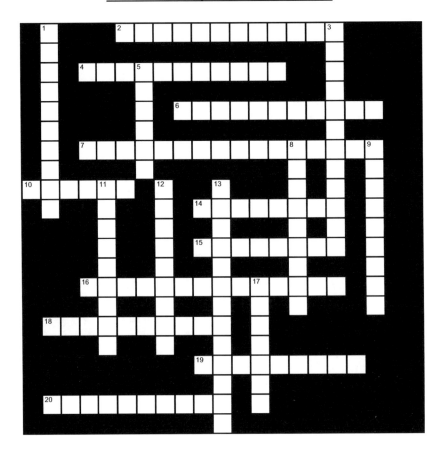

**Across**

2. What covers the axon? (12)
4. What does the trigeminal nerve control the muscles of? (11)
6. What is found on the outside of the spinal cord? (11)
7. Part of the brain stem (16)
10. Which plexus supplies the lower part of the abdominal wall and thigh? (6)
14. What part of the brain is divided into the left and right hemispheres? (8)
15. What is made up of dura mater, pia mater and arachnoid mater? (8)
16. Gaps in the myelin sheath, that help to increase the speed at which impulses are carried from one neurone to another (14)
18. Part of the nervous system that is concerned with all nerves outside the central nervous system (10)
19. Centre of the medulla oblongata regulating the constriction and dilation of blood vessels (9)
20. A disease caused by damage to the basal ganglia of the brain (10)

**Down**

1. What part of the brain regulates the balance of the body? (10)
3. Part of the brain that regulates the autonomic nervous system (12)
5. Where can the sensory receptors of the facial nerve be found? (6)
8. A type of nervous tissue (9)
9. What mater lies under the dura mater? (9)
11. Which nervous system is divided into the sympathetic and parasympathetic systems? (9)
12. Midbrain, pons varolii, medulla oblongata (9)
13. A disorder caused by damage to the brain of a baby during pregnancy (13)
17. What type of tissue is the nervous system made of? (7)

# The Nervous System – Crossword 5

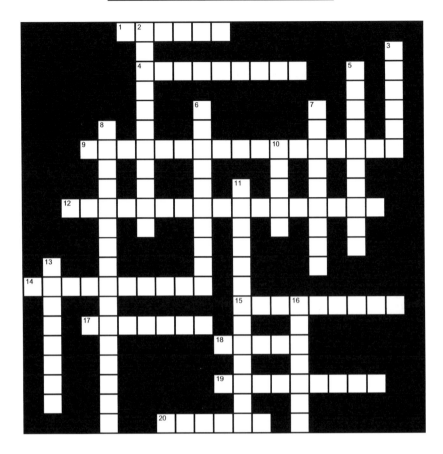

**Across**

1. Nerves which are divided into branches to form plexuses (6)

4. What does cerebrospinal fluid transport to the nerve cells? (9)

9. Chemicals which are released by nerve endings to allow the impulse to move from one neurone to another (17)

12. What disease of the central nervous system results in the loss of the myelin sheath covering the nerve fibres? (17)

14. A process whereby the body gets the energy it needs from food (10)

15. Plexus which supplies the skin and muscles of the pelvic area (9)

17. What part of the peripheral nervous system contains the spinal and cranial nerves? (7)

18. Efferent neurones (5)

19. What gland does the hypothalamus regulate? (9)

20. An action of pulling your hand away from a hot surface (6)

**Down**

2. Part of the brain stem (11)
3. Tiny fibrils (6)
5. What type of tissue are neuroglia made of? (10)
6. What part of the brain helps co-ordinate muscles? (10)
7. Nervous system that controls the automatic movements of smooth and cardiac muscle (9)
8. What part of the brain controls the heart and respiration? (16)
10. A type of neurone (5)
11. A neurotransmitter produced by neurons (13)
13. Part of a neurone (8)
16. Type of muscle which is controlled by the autonomic nervous system (7)

## Multiple Choice Answers – The Nervous System

| | | | | | | | | | | |
|---|---|---|---|---|---|---|---|---|---|---|
| 1 | B | 21 | B | 41 | D | 61 | C | 81 | A |
| 2 | C | 22 | D | 42 | C | 62 | D | | |
| 3 | A | 23 | D | 43 | C | 63 | C | | |
| 4 | B | 24 | A | 44 | A | 64 | D | | |
| 5 | A | 25 | C | 45 | D | 65 | B | | |
| 6 | A | 26 | B | 46 | C | 66 | A | | |
| 7 | B | 27 | B | 47 | A | 67 | B | | |
| 8 | D | 28 | C | 48 | C | 68 | D | | |
| 9 | D | 29 | A | 49 | A | 69 | A | | |
| 10 | C | 30 | D | 50 | A | 70 | B | | |
| 11 | C | 31 | A | 51 | D | 71 | B | | |
| 12 | A | 32 | A | 52 | D | 72 | A | | |
| 13 | A | 33 | A | 53 | B | 73 | D | | |
| 14 | B | 34 | D | 54 | C | 74 | C | | |
| 15 | C | 35 | B | 55 | B | 75 | A | | |
| 16 | D | 36 | C | 56 | A | 76 | D | | |
| 17 | B | 37 | C | 57 | C | 77 | D | | |
| 18 | B | 38 | A | 58 | C | 78 | B | | |
| 19 | B | 39 | B | 59 | A | 79 | D | | |
| 20 | C | 40 | D | 60 | B | 80 | D | | |

## Crossword Answers – The Nervous System

### Crossword 1

**Across**
3. Pons Varolii
7. Axon
8. Midbrain
12. Central
13. Sensory
14. Phrenic
15. Meninges

**Down**
1. Somatic
2. Brachial
4. Ventricles
5. Maxillary
6. Cerebellum
9. Cerebrum
10. Neuritis
11. Synapse

### Crossword 2

**Across**
1. Bell's Palsy
4. Cerebrum
5. Motor
6. Neuroglia
11. Pia Mater
12. Sympathetic
13. Sciatica
14. Sacral
15. Reflex

**Down**
2. Skeletal
3. Thoracic
7. Grey Matter
8. Ganglia
9. Dendrites
10. Opthalmic

## Crossword 3

**Across**
1. End Feet
3. Mandibular
7. Cranium
8. Neurones
12. Mixed
13. Oxytocin
14. Sensory

**Down**
2. Neurilemma
4. Dura Mater
5. Hypothalamus
6. Spinal
9. Shoulder
10. Fibrous
11. Brain

## Crossword 4

**Across**
2. Myelin Sheath
4. Mastication
6. White Matter
7. Medulla Oblongata
10. Lumbar
14. Cerebrum
15. Meninges
16. Nodes of Ranvier
18. Peripheral
19. Vasomotor
20. Parkinson's

**Down**
1. Cerebellum
3. Hypothalamus
5. Tongue
8. Neuroglia
9. Arachnoid
11. Autonomic
12. Brain Stem
13. Cerebral Palsy
17. Nervous

## Crossword 5

**Across**
1. Spinal
4. Nutrients
9. Neurotransmitters
12. Multiple Sclerosis
14. Metabolism
15. Coccygeal
17. Somatic
18. Motor
19. Pituitary
20. Reflex

**Down**
2. Pons Varolii
3. Fibres
5. Connective
6. Cerebellum
7. Autonomic
8. Medulla Oblongata
10. Mixed
11. Acetylcholine
13. Cell Body
16. Cardiac

# Chapter 9 | The Reproductive System

## Multiple Choice Questions

| | |
|---|---|
| **1. Where is the prostate gland situated?**<br>a) Above the bladder<br>b) Below the bladder and above the base of the penis<br>c) Between the urethra and testis<br>d) Below the vas deferens and above the ureter<br><br>*Answer:* _____ | **2. Which part of the male reproductive system passes sperm from the epididymis to the urethra?**<br>a) Prostate gland<br>b) Penis<br>c) Ureter<br>d) Vas deferens<br><br>*Answer:* _____ |
| **3. What is the position of the scrotum?**<br>a) Above the penis<br>b) Below the penis<br>c) Behind the penis<br>d) In front of the penis<br><br><br>*Answer:* _____ | **4. What is the first part of the birth canal?**<br>a) Uterus<br>b) Cervix<br>c) Vagina<br>d) Fallopian tubes<br><br><br>*Answer:* _____ |
| **5. Which one of the following is not a cause of amenorrhoea?**<br>a) Congestion of the uterus<br>b) Hormone imbalances<br>c) Extreme weight loss<br>d) Considerable amounts of exercise<br><br>*Answer:* _____ | **6. Where are the testes positioned?**<br>a) Between the bladder and epididymis<br>b) At the top of the urethra<br>c) At the start of the ureter<br>d) Within the scrotum<br><br><br>*Answer:* _____ |
| **7. The flagellum is another term for;**<br>a) Tip of the penis<br>b) Foreskin<br>c) Tail of a sperm cell<br>d) Head of a sperm cell<br><br><br>*Answer:* _____ | **8. The embryo becomes the foetus after how long?**<br>a) At the beginning of the $8^{th}$ week<br>b) At the beginning of the $10^{th}$ week<br>c) At the end of the $8^{th}$ week<br>d) At the end of the $9^{th}$ week<br><br>*Answer:* _____ |

| | |
|---|---|
| **9. Mature follicles are known as;**<br>a) Ovum<br>b) Graafian follicles<br>c) Fallopian tubes<br>d) Female sex cells<br><br><br>*Answer:* _____ | **10. What is the function of the pelvic girdle?**<br>a) Maintains shape<br>b) Heat<br>c) Protection<br>d) Protects the abdominal muscles<br><br>*Answer:* _____ |
| **11. Where does the epididymis begin?**<br>a) Below the scrotum<br>b) At the end of the prostate gland<br>c) At the top rear of each testis<br>d) Between the urethra and bladder<br><br><br><br>*Answer:* _____ | **12. Which part of the female reproductive system opens into the vagina?**<br>a) Uterus<br>b) Fallopian tube<br>c) Ovaries<br>d) Cervix<br><br>*Answer:* _____ |
| **13. What is the proper term for a ball of cells?**<br>a) Morula<br>b) Zygote<br>c) Foetus<br>d) Embryo<br><br>*Answer:* _____ | **14. The onset of menstruation is known as;**<br>a) Amenorrhoea<br>b) Dysmenorrhoea<br>c) Post menstrual syndrome<br>d) Pre menstrual syndrome<br><br>*Answer:* _____ |
| **15. A pregnancy that occurs outside the uterus is called;**<br>a) Polycystic ovarian syndrome<br>b) Ectopic pregnancy<br>c) Dysmenorrhoea<br>d) Amenorrhoea<br><br><br>*Answer:* _____ | **16. Which one of the following is not a function of the scrotum?**<br>a) To store sperm<br>b) To support the testes<br>c) To protect the testes<br>d) To keep the testes at a lower temperature than the rest of the body<br><br>*Answer:* _____ |
| **17. What are the male gonads called?**<br>a) Prostate gland<br>b) Epididymis<br>c) Testes<br>d) Testicular vessels<br><br><br>*Answer:* _____ | **18. What is the function of the urethra?**<br>a) To store sperm<br>b) To act as a passageway for urine and semen<br>c) To protect the glans<br>d) To store immature sperm cells<br><br>*Answer:* _____ |

| | |
|---|---|
| **19. How many chromosomes does the head of the sperm contain?**<br>a) 46<br>b) 12<br>c) 18<br>d) 23<br><br>*Answer:* _____ | **20. Extremely painful menstruation is known as;**<br>a) Amenorrhoea<br>b) Pre menstrual syndrome<br>c) Dysmenorrhoea<br>d) Polycystic ovarian syndrome<br><br>*Answer:* _____ |
| **21. What is not part of the pelvic girdle?**<br>a) Hip bones<br>b) Sacrum<br>c) Femur<br>d) Symphysis pubis<br><br><br>*Answer:* _____ | **22. What is the function of the epididymis?**<br>a) To produce sperm<br>b) To support the testes<br>c) To protect the testes<br>d) A reservoir for immature sperm cells<br><br>*Answer:* _____ |
| **23. What is not part of the penis?**<br>a) Ureter<br>b) Erectile tissue<br>c) Foreskin<br>d) Urethra<br><br>*Answer:* _____ | **24. What is a zygote?**<br>a) A ball of cells<br>b) A fluid filled sac<br>c) Tail of the sperm<br>d) First single cell of an individual<br><br>*Answer:* _____ |
| **25. Which one of the following is not part of the vulva?**<br>a) Mons pubis<br>b) Labia majora<br>c) Glans<br>d) Clitoris<br><br><br>*Answer:* _____ | **26. What is the function of the placenta?**<br>a) To secrete milk, post pregnancy<br>b) To allow the passage of nutrients to the baby and waste elimination from the baby<br>c) To break down the tail of the sperm after fertilisation<br>d) To enable the foetus to move<br><br>*Answer:* _____ |
| **27. Which one of the following is an effect of polycystic ovarian syndrome?**<br>a) Ovarian cysts<br>b) Bloating<br>c) Water retention<br>d) Restlessness<br><br><br><br>*Answer:* _____ | **28. Which one of the following is not a function of the pelvic girdle?**<br>a) Produces secretions<br>b) Protects the internal reproductive organs<br>c) Supports the vertebral column<br>d) Provides attachments for muscles of posture<br><br>*Answer:* _____ |

| 29. A walnut sized gland located in the pelvic area;<br>a) Testicular vessel<br>b) Prostate<br>c) Epididymis<br>d) Scrotum<br><br>Answer: _____ | 30. What is the structure of the scrotum?<br>a) Connective tissue<br>b) Skin and adipose tissue<br>c) Skin and muscle<br>d) Muscle and areolar tissue<br><br>Answer: _____ |
|---|---|
| 31. What is the position of the urethra in the male reproductive system?<br>a) Tip of the penis<br>b) Centre of the penis<br>c) Below the scrotum<br>d) Inside the scrotum<br><br>Answer: _____ | 32. The female sex cells are called;<br>a) Ova<br>b) Sperm<br>c) Glans<br>d) Ovaries<br><br>Answer: _____ |
| 33. Where does fertilization take place in the female reproductive system?<br>a) Uterus<br>b) Fallopian tubes<br>c) Urethra<br>d) Ovaries<br><br>Answer: _____ | 34. Where are the ovaries positioned?<br>a) Above the fallopian tubes<br>b) Each side of the uterus<br>c) Inside the uterus<br>d) At the top of the uterus<br><br>Answer: _____ |
| 35. Breasts are made up of;<br>a) Connective and muscular tissue<br>b) Elastic and adipose tissue<br>c) Adipose and connective tissue<br>d) Muscular tissue<br><br>Answer: _____ | 36. Amenorrhoea can be defined as;<br>a) Painful menstruation<br>b) Absence of menstruation<br>c) Irregular menstruation<br>d) Heavy menstruation<br><br>Answer: _____ |
| 37. What is the function of the prostate gland?<br>a) To store and produce seminal fluid<br>b) To maintain the correct temperature<br>c) It carries sperm to the testes<br>d) To support the testes<br><br>Answer: _____ | 38. What is the function of the uterus in the female reproductive system?<br>a) To secrete female hormones<br>b) To receive a fertilised ovum from the fallopian tube<br>c) Acts as a passageway for menstrual blood<br>d) Forms the first channel for the birth canal<br><br>Answer: _____ |

| | |
|---|---|
| **39. Childbirth usually occurs;**<br>a) In the 35th week of pregnancy<br>b) In the 40th week of pregnancy<br>c) In the 42nd week of pregnancy<br>d) In the 30th week of pregnancy<br><br><br>*Answer:* _____ | **40. What is the cause of virilism in females?**<br>a) Hypersecretion of luteinising hormone<br>b) Hypersecretion of testosterone<br>c) Hyposecretion of female sex hormones<br>d) Hyposecretion of testosterone<br><br>*Answer:* _____ |
| **41. Where does the foetus develop?**<br>a) Birth canal<br>b) Placenta<br>c) Ureter<br>d) Amniotic cavity<br><br><br><br><br>*Answer:* _____ | **42. What is the structure of the uterus?**<br>a) A thin muscular hollow tube<br>b) An organ made of elastic tissue<br>c) A muscular passageway from the cervix to the vulva<br>d) A small hollow organ with thick muscular walls<br><br>*Answer:* _____ |
| **43. What part of the male reproductive system leads from the epididymis to the urethra?**<br>a) Prostate gland<br>b) Vas deferens<br>c) Ureter<br>d) Erectile tissue<br><br>*Answer:* _____ | **44. What part of the male reproductive system produces testosterone?**<br>a) Epididymis<br>b) Testes<br>c) Prostate gland<br>d) Urethra<br><br><br><br>*Answer:* _____ |
| **45. The womb is also called;**<br>a) Follicle<br>b) Cervix<br>c) Uterus<br>d) Vulva<br><br>*Answer:* _____ | **46. What do graafian follicles contain?**<br>a) The ovum<br>b) Tissue and fluid<br>c) Vulva and fluid<br>d) Nerve endings<br><br>*Answer:* _____ |
| **47. What is the structure of fallopian tubes?**<br>a) Hollow tubes<br>b) Muscular hollow tubes<br>c) Very fine funnel shaped tubes<br>d) Tightly coiled tubes<br><br><br>*Answer:* _____ | **48. The vulva can be defined as;**<br>a) The external genitalia of the female reproductive system<br>b) The internal genitalia of the female reproductive system<br>c) Mature follicles<br>d) Female sex cells<br><br><br>*Answer:* _____ |

| | |
|---|---|
| **49. Extremely painful menstruation is known as;**<br>a) Dysmenorrhoea<br>b) Polycystic ovarian syndrome<br>c) Menarche<br>d) Amenorrhoea<br><br>*Answer:* _____ | **50. Which part of the male reproductive system produces sperm cells?**<br>a) Testes<br>b) Prostate gland<br>c) Scrotum<br>d) Epididymis<br><br>*Answer:* _____ |
| **51. Which one of the following is contained within the scrotum?**<br>a) Testes<br>b) Erectile tissue<br>c) Seminal fluid<br>d) Prostate<br><br>*Answer:* _____ | **52. Which one of the following is a function of the penis?**<br>a) To produce testosterone<br>b) Organ of reproduction<br>c) To protect the testes<br>d) Storage<br><br>*Answer:* _____ |
| **53. Which part of the male reproductive system fertilises the female egg?**<br>a) Prostate gland<br>b) Sperm<br>c) Penis<br>d) Glans<br><br>*Answer:* _____ | **54. Which one of the following is a function of the ovaries?**<br>a) Storage of oestrogen and progesterone<br>b) Site of fertilisation<br>c) Acts as a passageway for menstrual blood<br>d) Secretes oestrogen and progesterone<br><br>*Answer:* _____ |
| **55. What part of the vulva protects the clitoris?**<br>a) Mons pubis<br>b) Labia minora<br>c) Labia majora<br>d) Vagina<br><br>*Answer:* _____ | **56. What is the structure of the vas deferens?**<br>a) A small gland positioned behind the scrotum<br>b) A tightly coiled gland<br>c) A tube with muscular walls<br>d) A sac made of skin and muscle<br><br>*Answer:* _____ |
| **57. The prepuce is another term for;**<br>a) Foreskin<br>b) Tip of the penis<br>c) Erectile tissue<br>d) Sperm<br><br>*Answer:* _____ | **58. What is the uterus lined with;**<br>a) Endometrium<br>b) Fibrous tissue<br>c) Graafian follicle<br>d) Placenta<br><br>*Answer:* _____ |

| | |
|---|---|
| **59. Where are the female sex cells stored?**<br><br>a) Uterus<br>b) Cervix<br>c) Ovaries<br>d) Vagina<br><br><br>*Answer:* _____ | **60. What is the function of the labia majora?**<br><br>a) To protect the other external female reproductive organs<br>b) To protect the symphysis pubis<br>c) To protect the clitoris<br>d) To protect the labia minora<br><br>*Answer:* _____ |
| **61. Where do immature sperm cells develop?**<br><br>a) Epididymis<br>b) Vas deferens<br>c) Scrotum<br>d) Testes<br><br><br>*Answer:* _____ | **62. The glans is another term for;**<br><br>a) Foreskin<br>b) Spermatoza<br>c) Tip of the penis<br>d) Testes<br><br><br><br>*Answer:* _____ |
| **63. What are the female gonads called?**<br><br>a) Ovaries<br>b) Eggs<br>c) Testes<br>d) Fallopian tubes<br><br><br><br><br><br>*Answer:* _____ | **64. Which one of the following is not a function of the vagina?**<br><br>a) Acts as a passageway for menstrual flow<br>b) Forms the first part of the birth canal<br>c) Site of penetration during intercourse<br>d) Connects the internal genitalia with the external genitalia<br><br><br>*Answer:* _____ |
| **65. What is the function of the mons pubis?**<br><br>a) To protect the entrance to the vagina<br>b) Form a hood to protect the clitoris<br>c) To form part of the birth canal<br>d) To protect the symphysis pubis<br><br>*Answer:* _____ | |

# The Reproductive System - Crossword 1

## Across

1. Part of the body which protects the female reproductive organs (12)
5. A small gland of the male reproductive system situated between the bladder and rectum (8)
6. Where does the foetus grow and develop? (6)
8. What fertilises the ova? (5)
10. Female sex cells (3)
13. Where is the prostate gland positioned? (7)
14. A sac which holds the testes (7)

## Down

2. A passageway for sperm (11)
3. Painful menstruation (13)
4. What part of the female reproductive system opens into the vagina? (6)
7. Tail of the sperm (9)
9. A mass of cells (6)
11. Tip of the penis (5)
12. Glands of the male reproductive system (6)

## The Reproductive System - Crossword 2

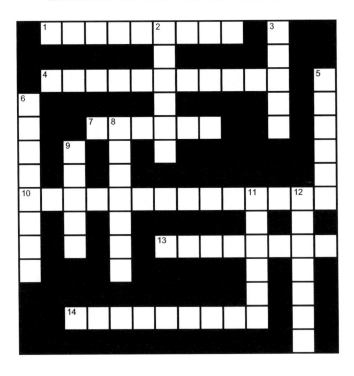

**Across**

1. Small structures on the surface of the ovary (9)
4. Giving birth (11)
7. What connects the cervix to the vulva? (6)
10. Where does the fertilisation of the ovum occur? (14)
13. Baby's support system (8)
14. A protective pad of fat over the symphysis pubis (9)

**Down**

2. The neck of the uterus (6)
3. Male organ of excretion (5)
5. What is the embryo known as from 8 weeks? (6)
6. Mature follicles (8)
8. A type of breast tissue (7)
9. What is the labia majora part of? (5)
11. The womb (6)
12. Pregnancy which occurs outside the uterus (7)

# The Reproductive System – Crossword 3

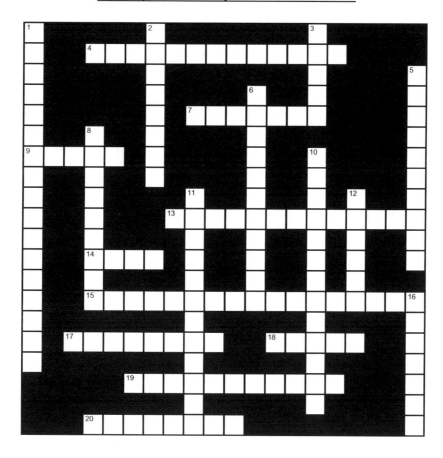

**Across**

4. Difficult menstruation (13)
7. Accessory organs of the female reproductive system (7)
9. What is released through the vas deferens? (5)
13. What occurs when the sperm penetrates the inner membrane of the ovum? (13)
14. A single egg (4)
15. Part of the male reproductive system (17)
17. A fold of skin called the prepuce (8)
18. External genitals of the female reproductive system (5)
19. What does the epididymis open up into? (11)
20. The area, in the male reproductive system, between the anus and sex organs (8)

**Down**

1. A syndrome caused by the hyposecretion of female sex hormones (17)
2. A cavity which contains the embryo (8)
3. What part of the male reproductive system acts as a passageway for semen? (5)
5. The passageway from the uterus to the outside of the vagina through which the fetus passes during child birth (10)
6. What part of the vulva protects the clitoris (11)
8. A function of the epididymis (9)
10. Gland that produces thin, milky fluid to help semen travel along the urethra more easily (13)
11. What protects the internal organs of the reproductive systems? (12)
12. What part of the female reproductive system is the cervix part of? (6)
16. A function of the scrotum (7)

## Multiple Choice Answers – The Reproductive System

| | | | | | | | |
|----|---|----|---|----|---|----|---|
| 1 | B | 21 | C | 41 | D | 61 | A |
| 2 | D | 22 | D | 42 | D | 62 | C |
| 3 | B | 23 | A | 43 | B | 63 | A |
| 4 | B | 24 | D | 44 | B | 64 | B |
| 5 | A | 25 | C | 45 | C | 65 | D |
| 6 | D | 26 | B | 46 | A | | |
| 7 | C | 27 | A | 47 | C | | |
| 8 | C | 28 | A | 48 | A | | |
| 9 | B | 29 | B | 49 | A | | |
| 10 | C | 30 | C | 50 | A | | |
| 11 | C | 31 | B | 51 | A | | |
| 12 | D | 32 | A | 52 | B | | |
| 13 | A | 33 | B | 53 | B | | |
| 14 | D | 34 | B | 54 | D | | |
| 15 | B | 35 | C | 55 | B | | |
| 16 | A | 36 | B | 56 | C | | |
| 17 | C | 37 | A | 57 | A | | |
| 18 | B | 38 | B | 58 | A | | |
| 19 | D | 39 | B | 59 | C | | |
| 20 | C | 40 | C | 60 | A | | |

## Crossword Answers – The Reproductive System

### Crossword 1

**Across**
1. Pelvic Girdle
5. Prostate
6. Uterus
8. Sperm
10. Ova
13. Urethra
14. Scrotum

**Down**
2. Vas Deferens
3. Dysmenorrhoea
4. Cervix
7. Flagellum
9. Morula
11. Glans
12. Testes

### Crossword 2

**Across**
1. Follicles
4. Parturition
7. Vagina
10. Fallopian Tubes
13. Placenta
14. Mons Pubis

**Down**
2. Cervix
3. Penis
5. Foetus
6. Graafian
8. Areolar
9. Vulva
11. Uterus
12. Ectopic

## Crossword 3

| Across | Down |
|--------|------|
| 4. Dysmenorrhoea | 1. Polycystic Ovarian |
| 7. Breasts | 2. Amniotic |
| 9. Sperm | 3. Penis |
| 13. Fertilisation | 5. Birth Canal |
| 14. Ovum | 6. Labia Minora |
| 15. Testicular Vessels | 8. Transport |
| 17. Foreskin | 10. Prostate Gland |
| 18. Vulva | 11. Pelvic Girdle |
| 19. Vas Deferens | 12. Uterus |
| 20. Perineum | 16. Support |

# Chapter 10 | The Digestive System

## Multiple Choice Questions

| | |
|---|---|
| **1. How many pairs of salivary glands are there?**<br>a) 1<br>b) 4<br>c) 2<br>d) 3<br><br>*Answer:* _____ | **2. Where is the submandibular gland situated?**<br>a) Above the ear<br>b) Below the ear<br>c) Below the tongue<br>d) Above the tongue<br><br>*Answer:* _____ |
| **3. What is the function of bile?**<br>a) The breakdown of proteins<br>b) The breakdown of glycerol<br>c) The breakdown of bacteria<br>d) To break down fats<br><br>*Answer:* _____ | **4. Peptones are broken down into;**<br>a) Proteins<br>b) Peptidases<br>c) Polypeptides<br>d) Amino acids<br><br>*Answer:* _____ |
| **5. Where is the gall bladder positioned?**<br>a) Behind the liver<br>b) In front of the liver<br>c) To the left of the liver<br>d) To the right of the liver<br><br><br>*Answer:* _____ | **6. A break in the walls of the digestive system causes;**<br>a) Jaundice<br>b) Ulcers<br>c) Hernia<br>d) Gall stones<br><br>*Answer:* _____ |
| **7. What is the function of insulin?**<br>a) To convert glucose back to glycogen<br>b) To regulate the production of vitamins A, B12, D, E, K<br>c) To regulate blood sugar levels<br>d) To regulate body temperature<br><br>*Answer:* _____ | **8. Chemical digestion of food is completed;**<br>a) In the large intestine<br>b) In the stomach<br>c) In the small intestine<br>d) In the oesophagus<br><br>*Answer:* _____ |

| | |
|---|---|
| **9. What is the function of peptidases?**<br>a) Breaks polypeptides up into amino acids<br>b) Produces trypsin in pancreatic juice<br>c) Breaks proteins up into peptones<br>d) Breaks disaccharides up into monosaccharides<br><br>*Answer:* _____ | **10. The bolus is described as;**<br>a) The process of digestion<br>b) A chemical catalyst<br>c) The ball of food that is pushed from the back of the mouth down into the oesophagus<br>d) An enzyme which changes the polysaccharides into disaccharides<br><br>*Answer:* _____ |
| **11. Which one of the following is not a layer of the small intestinal wall?**<br>a) A layer of blood vessels<br>b) A layer of fibrous tissue<br>c) A muscular layer<br>d) A layer of lymph vessels<br><br>*Answer:* _____ | **12. An obstruction in a bile duct causes;**<br>a) Hernia<br>b) Cirrhosis<br>c) Gall stones<br>d) Jaundice<br><br>*Answer:* _____ |
| **13. Where is the pancreas located?**<br>a) Behind the stomach<br>b) Behind the liver<br>c) Posterior stomach<br>d) Under the duodenum<br><br>*Answer:* _____ | **14. What is the largest gland in the body?**<br>a) Liver<br>b) Gall bladder<br>c) Pancreas<br>d) Stomach<br><br>*Answer:* _____ |
| **15. How long is the large intestine?**<br>a) 2.5m<br>b) 1.5m<br>c) 1.5cm<br>d) 1m<br><br>*Answer:* _____ | **16. What organ secretes intestinal juices?**<br>a) Small intestine<br>b) Liver<br>c) Gall bladder<br>d) Pancreas<br><br>*Answer:* _____ |
| **17. What is the function of hydrochloric acid?**<br>a) Emulsifies fats<br>b) Kills harmful bacteria<br>c) Changes proteins into peptones<br>d) Changes polypeptides into amino acids<br><br>*Answer:* _____ | **18. Which part of the digestive system is responsible for carbohydrate and fat digestion?**<br>a) Stomach<br>b) Small intestine<br>c) Large intestine<br>d) Liver<br><br>*Answer:* _____ |

| | |
|---|---|
| **19. Which one of the following is not a function of saliva?**<br>a) To lubricate food when swallowing<br>b) To clean the mouth and teeth<br>c) To begin digestion<br>d) To aid chemical digestion<br><br>*Answer:* _____ | **20. What is the principal organ of digestion?**<br>a) Stomach<br>b) Oesophagus<br>c) Small intestine<br>d) Large intestine<br><br>*Answer:* _____ |
| **21. Which of the following is not a function of the tongue?**<br>a) Taste<br>b) To carry chewed food from the mouth to the stomach<br>c) Chewing<br>d) Swallowing<br><br>*Answer:* _____ | **22. How long is the small intestine?**<br>a) 12.5m<br>b) 9m<br>c) 7m<br>d) 1.5m<br><br><br><br><br>*Answer:* _____ |
| **23. What are the accessory organs involved in the digestion process are?**<br>a) Liver and pancreas<br>b) Pancreas and gall bladder<br>c) Liver, pancreas and duodenum<br>d) Liver, gall bladder and pancreas<br><br>*Answer:* _____ | **24. Pancreatic juice contains which one of the following enzymes?**<br>a) Lipase<br>b) Fibrinogen<br>c) Albumin<br>d) Globulin<br><br><br>*Answer:* _____ |
| **25. The stomach is responsible for which type of digestion?**<br>a) Protein digestion<br>b) Fat digestion<br>c) Carbohydrate digestion<br>d) Fat and carbohydrate digestion<br><br>*Answer:* _____ | **26. Saliva contains;**<br>a) Salt, water and bile<br>b) Water, mucus and enzymes<br>c) Water and enzymes<br>d) Water, mucus and hydrochloric acid<br><br><br><br>*Answer:* _____ |
| **27. Which enzyme curdles milk?**<br>a) Pepsin<br>b) Peptones<br>c) Peptidase<br>d) Rennin<br><br>*Answer:* _____ | **28. A simple sugar is known as;**<br>a) Monosaccharide<br>b) Polysaccharide<br>c) Saccharide<br>d) Disaccharide<br><br>*Answer:* _____ |

| | |
|---|---|
| **29. What is the function of the large intestine?**<br>a) Kills harmful bacteria<br>b) Churns food with intestinal juices<br>c) To remove any water and nutrients from digestive waste<br>d) Absorb alcohol<br><br>*Answer: _____* | **30. Which one of the following is not stored by the liver?**<br>a) Iron<br>b) Vitamin E<br>c) Glycogen<br>d) Vitamin B6<br><br><br>*Answer: _____* |
| **31. Gall stones are caused from a build up of;**<br>a) Bile pigments, fats and salts<br>b) Cholesterol and bile<br>c) Bile pigments and cholesterol<br>d) Cholesterol and calcium deposits<br><br><br><br><br><br>*Answer: _____* | **32. What is the function of the oesophagus?**<br>a) To push the ball of food into the back of the mouth<br>b) To produce mucus to lubricate food<br>c) To eliminate nutrients from digestive waste<br>d) To convey chewed food downwards towards the stomach<br><br>*Answer: _____* |
| **33. Which one of the following is not part of the large intestine?**<br>a) Colon<br>b) Appendix<br>c) Rectum<br>d) Ileum<br><br>*Answer: _____* | **34. Where is bile stored?**<br>a) Pancreas<br>b) Liver<br>c) Gall bladder<br>d) Stomach<br><br><br>*Answer: _____* |
| **35. Which salivary gland is situated below the ear?**<br>a) Parotid gland<br>b) Sublingual gland<br>c) Zygomatic gland<br>d) Submandibular gland<br><br>*Answer: _____* | **36. What is the function of the epiglottis?**<br>a) To digest proteins and carbohydrates<br>b) To prevent choking<br>c) Aids mastication<br>d) To lubricate the food with water and mucus<br><br>*Answer: _____* |

| | |
|---|---|
| **37. What is the function of the enzyme lipase?**<br>a) To change fats into fatty acids and glycerol<br>b) To change peptones into polypeptides<br>c) Breaks down milk into curds<br>d) To change starch into polysaccharides<br><br>*Answer:* _____ | **38. Which one of the following is not a function of the large intestine?**<br>a) Defecation<br>b) Absorption of alcohol<br>c) Storage of faeces<br>d) Production of mucus to help passage of faeces<br><br>*Answer:* _____ |
| **39. What produces insulin?**<br>a) Gall bladder<br>b) Islets of langerhans<br>c) Pancreatic duct<br>d) Bile<br><br><br><br><br><br><br><br>*Answer:* _____ | **40. What is the function of glucagon?**<br>a) To convert glucose to glycogen increasing blood sugar levels<br>b) To convert glycogen into glucose thereby raising blood sugar levels in the blood<br>c) To increase blood sugar levels allowing more nutrients to reach various organs<br>d) To help with the production of pancreatic juice<br><br>*Answer:* _____ |
| **41. Food passes from the pharynx to;**<br>a) Large intestine<br>b) Stomach<br>c) Oesophagus<br>d) Small intestine<br><br>*Answer:* _____ | **42. Gastric juices do not contain;**<br>a) Hydrochloric acid<br>b) Vitamin D<br>c) Rennin<br>d) Pepsin<br><br>*Answer:* _____ |
| **43. What is the structure of the stomach?**<br>a) A funnel shaped elastic organ<br>b) An elastic organ made of fibrous tissue<br>c) A hollow muscular organ which expands and contracts<br>d) A muscular organ made of fibrous tissue<br><br>*Answer:* _____ | **44. What makes up the small intestine?**<br>a) Oesophagus and duodenum<br>b) Duodenum, jejunum and oesophagus<br>c) Duodenum, hilium and ileum<br>d) Duodenum, jejunum and ileum<br><br><br><br>*Answer:* _____ |

**45. What is the function of bilirubin?**

a) To secrete mucus

b) To produce vitamin A

c) To give faeces its colour

d) Neutralises bacteria

Answer: _____

**46. Which of the following is a function of the gall bladder?**

a) Storage of bile

b) Converts glycogen to glucose

c) Elimination of waste materials

d) To store vitamins A, B, D, & E

Answer: _____

**47. What is a function of the pancreas?**

a) To produce a mucus for bile

b) To store saturated fat

c) To produce iron

d) To produce enzymes to help with food digestion

Answer: _____

**48. Which one of the following is not produced by the liver?**

a) Bile

b) Urea

c) Vitamin E

d) Heat

Answer: _____

**49. What is the large intestine responsible for?**

a) Breaking down fats

b) Elimination of waste

c) Converting protein into peptones

d) Lubricating food

Answer: _____

**50. What is the function of an enzyme?**

a) To begin the secretion of pancreatic juices

b) To speed up a chemical reaction

c) To complete the process of chemical digestion

d) To carry chewed food to the back of the mouth

Answer: _____

**51. The duodenum is the first part of which part of the digestive system?**

a) The stomach

b) Large intestine

c) Small intestine

d) Oesophagus

Answer: _____

**52. What is the function of salivary amylase?**

a) Begins the digestion of starch

b) Converts milk into curds

c) Changes fats into fatty acids

d) Begins the digestion of proteins

Answer: _____

**53. Which of the following is not a function of the stomach?**

a) Digestion of  proteins

b) Churn the food and mix it with gastric juices

c) The stomach produces vitamin A

d) Absorbs alcohol into the bloodstream

Answer: _____

**54. What is the function of the cardiac sphincter?**

a) To prevent choking

b) To control the movement of food into the stomach

c) To carry food to the small intestine

d) To carry food to the large intestine

Answer: _____

**55. A disaccharide is a type of;**
a) Pancreatic juice
b) Fat
c) Protein
d) Carbohydrate

Answer: _____

**56. What is an enzyme?**
a) A gastric juice in the stomach
b) A chemical compound
c) A chemical reaction
d) A chemical catalyst

Answer: _____

**57. What is the function of the small intestine?**
a) To absorb nutrients into the bloodstream
b) To emulsify fats and carbohydrates
c) To remove waste
d) To begin the production of intestinal juices

Answer: _____

**58. Where is the liver positioned?**
a) Below the abdomen
b) The upper left hand side of the abdomen
c) The upper right hand side of the abdomen
d) At the right side of the abdomen

Answer: _____

**59. What enzyme splits proteins into peptones?**
a) Peptidase
b) Polypeptides
c) Trypsin
d) Pepsin

Answer: _____

**60. What is the function of enterokinase?**
a) Changes disaccharides into monosaccharides
b) Splits peptones into polypeptides
c) Emulsifies fatty acids
d) Changes trypsinogen into trypsin

Answer: _____

**61. Which one of the following is not a function of the liver?**
a) Secretion of bile
b) Removes toxins
c) Production of heat
d) Production of enzymes to break down food

Answer: _____

**62. How does food travel from the mouth to the stomach?**
a) Through the gall bladder
b) Through the small intestine
c) Through large intestine
d) Through the oesophagus

Answer: _____

**63. Food leaves the stomach through the;**
a) Pyloric sphincter
b) Cardiac sphincter
c) Oesophagus
d) Large intestine

Answer: _____

**64. Which enzyme is involved in protein digestion?**
a) Histamine
b) Trypsin
c) Globulin
d) Bile

Answer: _____

**65. Where are taste buds located?**
a) On the tongue
b) In saliva
c) Oesophagus
d) Lips

*Answer:* _____

## The Digestive System - Crossword 1

**Across**

4. What does the liver store? (8)
7. What does the liver produce? (7)
8. A muscular organ in the mouth (6)
11. What enzyme begins the digestion of protein in the stomach? (6)
13. A process that takes place in the small intestine (10)
14. What part of the digestive system secretes gastric juices? (7)
15. A pancreatic juice (6)

**Down**

1. A liquid produced in the liver (4)
2. A gland which produces amylase (8)
3. A salivary gland (7)
5. An enzyme found in gastric juices (6)
6. Chemical catalysts (7)
9. Part of the small intestine (7)
10. An enzyme found in intestinal juices M_____ (7)
12. Protrusion of an organ through the abdominal wall (6)

# The Digestive System - Crossword 2

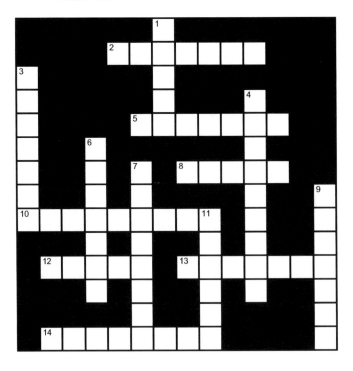

**Across**

2. What does the liver break down? (7)
5. A muscular tube which pushes the food into the oesophagus (7)
8. Found in saliva (5)
10. Damage to the liver often caused by alcohol (9)
12. A function of the tongue (5)
13. What does the liver detoxify? (7)
14. What does the liver store? (9)

**Down**

1. Where does digestion begin? (5)
3. Food exits the stomach through which sphincter? (7)
4. What does the small intestine protect the digestive system against? (9)
6. An enzyme which splits disaccharides into monosaccharides (7)
7. The first part of the small intestine (8)
9. Converts polysaccharides into disaccharides (7)
11. What keeps the mouth and teeth clean? (6)

## The Digestive System – Crossword 3

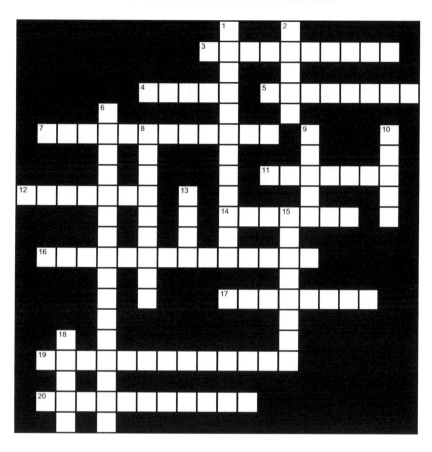

**Across**

3. What closes the larynx during swallowing to prevent food going down the wrong way? (10)
4. Visible folds on the walls of the stomach (5)
5. What part of the digestive system is located between the stomach and the jejunum? (8)
7. What does the enzyme pepsin break proteins down into? (12)
11. A sphincter which is positioned at the junction of the stomach (7)
12. Glycogen is broken down into what substance by the liver? (7)
14. What enzyme is involved in protein digestion? (7)
16. What does the duodenum, jejunum and ileum form? (14)
17. A psychological illness causing a loss of appetite (8)
19. A form of carbohydrates (13)
20. A muscular contraction which moves food along the alimentary canal (11)

**Down**

1. Inflammation of the appendix (12)
2. Part of the small intestine (5)
6. A substance contained within gastric juice that kills potential harmful bacteria (16)
8. Amino acids that the body cannot make (9)
9. The ball of food that is pushed to the back of the mouth (5)
10. What does the gall bladder secrete? (5)
13. What is produced by the liver? (4)
15. Where are trypsin, amylase and lipase produced? (8)
18. What organ stores vitamins A, D, E, K and B12? (5)

# The Digestive System – Crossword 4

**Across**

1. A burning pain in the foodpipe (9)
5. Islets of _____ (10)
6. Water soluble protein derivatives (8)
7. A bile pigment which gives faeces its colour (9)
10. A yellowing of the skin caused by excess bilirubin in the blood (8)
12. What enzyme is produced by cells in the duodenum wall (12)
14. Where can villi be found? (14)
16. A mineral which is stored by the liver (4)
17. Where is bile stored? (11)
18. Tiny projections on the tongue containing taste buds (8)
19. A hormone secreted by the pancreas (7)

**Down**

2. Part of the large intestine (8)
3. An enzyme involved in the digestion of carbohydrates (7)
4. A form of proteins which are absorbed directly into the bloodstream for metabolism (10)
8. What does hydrochloric acid kill? (8)
9. Found in bile (5)
11. The expulsion of faeces (11)
13. What substance is removed from amino acids by the liver? (8)
15. Lipase breaks down what substance into fatty acids and glycerol? (4)

## Multiple Choice Answers – The Digestive System

| | | | | | | | | |
|---|---|---|---|---|---|---|---|---|
| 1 | D | | 21 | B | | 41 | C | | 61 | D |
| 2 | C | | 22 | C | | 42 | B | | 62 | D |
| 3 | D | | 23 | D | | 43 | C | | 63 | A |
| 4 | C | | 24 | A | | 44 | D | | 64 | B |
| 5 | A | | 25 | A | | 45 | C | | 65 | A |
| 6 | B | | 26 | B | | 46 | A | | | |
| 7 | C | | 27 | D | | 47 | D | | | |
| 8 | C | | 28 | A | | 48 | C | | | |
| 9 | A | | 29 | C | | 49 | B | | | |
| 10 | C | | 30 | D | | 50 | C | | | |
| 11 | B | | 31 | C | | 51 | C | | | |
| 12 | D | | 32 | D | | 52 | A | | | |
| 13 | A | | 33 | D | | 53 | C | | | |
| 14 | A | | 34 | C | | 54 | B | | | |
| 15 | B | | 35 | A | | 55 | D | | | |
| 16 | A | | 36 | B | | 56 | D | | | |
| 17 | B | | 37 | A | | 57 | A | | | |
| 18 | B | | 38 | B | | 58 | C | | | |
| 19 | D | | 39 | B | | 59 | D | | | |
| 20 | A | | 40 | B | | 60 | D | | | |

## Crossword Answers

### Crossword 1

**Across**
4. Glycogen
7. Heparin
8. Tongue
11. Pepsin
13. Absorption
14. Stomach
15. Lipase

**Down**
1. Bile
2. Pancreas
3. Parotid
5. Rennin
6. Enzymes
9. Jejunum
10. Maltase
12. Hernia

### Crossword 2

**Across**
2. Protein
5. Pharynx
8. Water
10. Cirrhosis
12. Taste
13. Alcohol
14. Vitamin A

**Down**
1. Mouth
3. Cardiac
4. Infection
6. Sucrase
7. Duodenum
9. Amylase
11. Saliva

## Crossword 3

**Across**

3. Epiglottis
4. Rugae
5. Duodenum
7. Polypeptides
11. Pyloric
12. Glucose
14. Trypsin
16. Small Intestine
17. Anorexia
19. Disarccharides
20. Peristalsis

**Down**

1. Appendicitis
2. Ileum
6. Hydrochloric Acid
8. Essential
9. Bolus
10. Mucus
13. Heat
15. Pancreas
18. Liver

## Crossword 4

**Across**

1. Heartburn
5. Langerhans
6. Peptones
7. Bilirubin
10. Jaundice
12. Enterokinase
14. Small Intestine
16. Iron
17. Gall Bladder
18. Papillae
19. Insulin

**Down**

2. Appendix
3. Maltase
4. Amino Acids
8. Bacteria
9. Salts
11. Defaecation
13. Nitrogen
15. Fats

# Chapter 11 | The Respiratory System

## Multiple Choice Questions

| | |
|---|---|
| **1. The hollow spaces inside the bones of the skull surrounding the nose are called;**<br>a) Nasal bones<br>b) Nasal cavity<br>c) Nasal septum<br>d) Sinuses<br><br>*Answer:* _____ | **2. The alveoli arise from;**<br>a) Bronchioles<br>b) Bronchi<br>c) Pleural cavity<br>d) Larynx<br><br>*Answer:* _____ |
| **3. What is the pons varolii's role in breathing?**<br>a) Regulates inspiration<br>b) Starts Inspiration<br>c) Starts Expiration<br>d) Expands the diaphragm<br><br>*Answer:* _____ | **4. Which one of the following is not a function of the diaphragm?**<br>a) Inhalation<br>b) Parturition<br>c) Exhalation<br>d) Mastication<br><br>*Answer:* _____ |
| **5. What is the function of the pleural cavity?**<br>a) To prevent friction between the layers of the lungs<br>b) To exchange gases between the layers of the lungs<br>c) To prevent a backflow of air between the layers of the lungs<br>d) To moisten the layers of the lungs<br><br>*Answer:* _____ | **6. What leads to the respiratory bronchioles?**<br>a) Fibrous bronchioles<br>b) End bronchioles<br>c) Terminal bronchioles<br>d) Ciliated bronchioles<br><br><br>*Answer:* _____ |
| **7. What connects the trachea to the lungs?**<br>a) Larynx<br>b) Pharynx<br>c) Bronchioles<br>d) Bronchi<br><br>*Answer:* _____ | **8. What forms the adam's apple?**<br>a) Small masses of lymphoid tissue<br>b) The thyroid cartilage surrounding the larynx<br>c) Pharyngeal tonsils<br>d) Palatine tonsils<br><br>*Answer:* _____ |

| | |
|---|---|
| **9. Where are the palatine tonsils situated?**<br>a) Underneath the tongue<br>b) At the back of the throat on the right and left side<br>c) At the back of the larynx<br>d) Beneath the trachea<br><br>*Answer:* _____ | **10. What is the second passageway for air entering the body?**<br>a) Bronchi<br>b) Pharynx<br>c) Trachea<br>d) Larynx<br><br><br>*Answer:* _____ |
| **11. What is the structure of bronchi?**<br>a) Hyaline cartilage and smooth muscle<br>b) Hyaline cartilage and voluntary muscle<br>c) Hyaline cartilage and elastic tissue<br>d) Hyaline cartilage and cardiac muscle<br><br><br>*Answer:* _____ | **12. What is the function of the alveoli?**<br>a) To exchange gases<br>b) To moisten and warm the cilia of the lungs<br>c) The exchange of oxygen and carbon dioxide in the out of the blood<br>d) To pass air into the bronchioles<br><br>*Answer:* _____ |
| **13. Tuberculosis is caused by;**<br>a) Inflammation of the alveoli<br>b) An allergic reaction<br>c) Inflammation of the lungs<br>d) Bacterial infection<br><br>*Answer:* _____ | **14. What is the nose made of?**<br>a) Connective tissue<br>b) Cartilage<br>c) Elastic tissue<br>d) Muscular tissue<br><br>*Answer:* _____ |
| **15. The 2 airways of the nose are divided by;**<br>a) Nasal septum<br>b) Paranasal sinuses<br>c) Nasal cartilage<br>d) Nasal cavity<br><br>*Answer:* _____ | **16. Air travels from the pharynx to;**<br>a) Alveoli<br>b) Trachea<br>c) Bronchi<br>d) Larynx<br><br><br>*Answer:* _____ |
| **17. The trachea is also known as the;**<br>a) Voice box<br>b) Adam's apple<br>c) Windpipe<br>d) Enzyme<br><br><br>*Answer:* _____ | **18. Which part of the respiratory system is the final passageway of air from the nose to the lungs?**<br>a) Alveoli<br>b) Bronchi<br>c) Bronchioles<br>d) Pleura<br><br>*Answer:* _____ |

| | |
|---|---|
| **19. What is the inner layer of the pleura called?**<br>a) Parietal layer<br>b) Palatine layer<br>c) Visceral layer<br>d) Serous layer<br><br>*Answer:* _____ | **20. What is the chief muscle of respiration?**<br>a) Intercostal muscles<br>b) Rectus abdominis<br>c) Transverse abdominis<br>d) Diaphragm<br><br>*Answer:* _____ |
| **21. Inflammation of the lungs causes;**<br>a) Pleurisy<br>b) Emphysema<br>c) Pneumonia<br>d) Tuberculosis<br><br>*Answer:* _____ | **22. What is the first passageway for air?**<br>a) Nose<br>b) Larynx<br>c) Trachea<br>d) Bronchi<br><br>*Answer:* _____ |
| **23. The pharynx opens into the;**<br>a) Trachea and larynx<br>b) Oesophagus and trachea<br>c) Oesophagus and larynx<br>d) Trachea and bronchi<br><br><br><br><br><br>*Answer:* _____ | **24. What is the structure of the trachea?**<br>a) Incomplete rings of hyaline cartilage and voluntary muscle<br>b) Connective tissue<br>c) Muscular and connective tissue<br>d) Rings of hyaline cartilage and involuntary muscle<br><br>*Answer:* _____ |
| **25. What is the function of the lungs?**<br>a) To filter bacteria<br>b) To facilitate the exchange of oxygen and carbon dioxide in and of the blood<br>c) To warm the air<br>d) The exchange of gases<br><br>*Answer:* _____ | **26. Where are the alveoli situated?**<br>a) At the end of the bronchi<br>b) At the beginning of the bronchioles<br>c) At the end of the bronchioles<br>d) Inside the trachea<br><br><br><br>*Answer:* _____ |
| **27. What nerve cells send impulses to the respiratory centre of the brain to increase breathing?**<br>a) Chemoreceptors<br>b) Chemical receptors<br>c) Neuralgia<br>d) Stretch receptors<br><br>*Answer:* _____ | **28. Inflammation of the pleural lining is known as;**<br>a) Pleurisy<br>b) Pneumonia<br>c) Tuberculosis<br>d) Hay fever<br><br><br><br>*Answer:* _____ |

| | |
|---|---|
| **29. Where does the exchange of gases in the lungs take place?**<br>a) Trachea<br>b) Bronchioles<br>c) Bronchi<br>d) Alveoli<br><br>*Answer:* _____ | **30. What is the trachea lined with?**<br>a) Mucus membrane<br>b) Ciliated epithelium<br>c) Serous membrane<br>d) Squamous epithelial cells<br><br>*Answer:* _____ |
| **31.The outer layer of the pleura is called;**<br>a) Parietal layer<br>b) Visceral layer<br>c) Hilium<br>d) Squamous layer<br><br>*Answer:* _____ | **32. Defaecation is another term for;**<br>a) Giving birth<br>b) Inhalation<br>c) Discharge of urine<br>d) Discharge of faeces<br><br>*Answer:* _____ |
| **33. Where is the diaphragm positioned?**<br>a) Above the lungs<br>b) Between the chest cavity and abdominal cavity<br>c) Above the heart<br>d) Under the stomach<br><br><br>*Answer:* _____ | **34. The symptoms of hay fever include;**<br>a) Sneezing, runny nose and eyes and coughing<br>b) Sneezing, headaches, runny nose<br>c) Respiratory infections<br>d) Sneezing, runny nose and itchy, swollen eyes<br><br>*Answer:* _____ |
| **35. What is the function of bronchi?**<br>a) To exchange gases<br>b) To carry air from the trachea into the bronchioles<br>c) To begin inhalation<br>d) To filter bacteria<br><br>*Answer:* _____ | **36. Where are the intercostal muscles positioned?**<br>a) Above the ribs<br>b) Below the ribs<br>c) Between the ribs<br>d) Behind the ribs<br><br><br>*Answer:* _____ |
| **37. What are found at the back of the pharynx?**<br>a) Columnar epithelium<br>b) Bronchi<br>c) Bronchioles<br>d) Tonsils<br><br>*Answer:* _____ | **38. The trachea branches off to form;**<br>a) Bronchioles<br>b) Bronchi<br>c) Alveoli<br>d) Pleura<br><br><br>*Answer:* _____ |

**39. What part of the respiratory system carries air to the lungs from the trachea?**
a) Larynx
b) Oesophagus
c) Bronchi
d) Bronchioles

Answer: _____

**40. What do bronchioles arise from?**
a) Trachea
b) Alveoli
c) Terminal bronchioles
d) Bronchi

Answer: _____

**41. Gaseous exchange can be defined as;**
a) The exchange of air in and out of the body's cells
b) The exchange of air in and out of the body
c) The exhalation of air out of cells
d) The inhalation of air into the cells

Answer: _____

**42. Parturition is another term for;**
a) Expiration
b) Giving birth
c) Discharge of faeces
d) Discharge of urine

Answer: _____

**43. BCG vaccines are used to prevent which disease?**
a) Pneumonia
b) Tuberculosis
c) Rhinitis
d) Emphysema

Answer: _____

**44. Hay fever is mainly caused by;**
a) Respiratory infections
b) Allergic reactions to pollens and allergens
c) Sinus infections
d) Bacteria

Answer: _____

**45. What is the structure of the alveoli?**
a) A single layer of squamous epithelial cells
b) A thick layer of serous membrane
c) A thick layer of squamous epithelial cells lined with ciliated membrane
d) A thin layer of ciliated epithelial cells

Answer: _____

**46. What are the 2 layers of the pleura separated by?**
a) Pleura
b) Pleura membrane
c) Pleura septum
d) Pleural cavity

Answer: _____

**47. External respiration is another term for;**
a) Inhalation
b) Exhalation
c) Breathing
d) Exchange of gases

Answer: _____

**48. Which one of the following is not a function of the nose?**
a) Organ of smell
b) Moisten and warms the air
c) Filters dust, bacteria and foreign matter
d) Sensory organ

Answer: _____

| 49. What is the pharynx made of? | 50. Where is the larynx positioned? |
|---|---|
| a) Muscular and fibrous tissue<br>b) Elastic and fibrous tissue<br>c) Muscular and elastic tissue<br>d) Muscular and connective tissue<br><br>*Answer:* _____ | a) Between the pharynx and the trachea<br>b) Between the trachea and oesophagus<br>c) At the back of the trachea<br>d) Between the tongue and pharynx<br><br>*Answer:* _____ |
| **51. Which one of the following is a function of the larynx?**<br>a) To carry air from the trachea to the bronchi<br>b) To carry air from the trachea to the alveoli<br>c) To exchange gases<br>d) Produces vocal sound<br><br>*Answer:* _____ | **52. What is the function of the trachea?**<br>a) To carry air between the larynx and the bronchi<br>b) To secrete foreign matter<br>c) To warm and moisten the air in the lungs<br>d) To assist in voice production<br><br>*Answer:* _____ |
| **53. Which part of the respiratory system takes air to the alveoli of the lungs?**<br>a) Pleura<br>b) Bronchioles<br>c) Bronchi<br>d) Capillaries<br><br>*Answer:* _____ | **54. What are the lungs surrounded by?**<br>a) Goblet cells<br>b) A membrane called the pleura<br>c) Ciliated epithelium<br>d) Serous epithelium<br><br>*Answer:* _____ |
| **55. What is the structure of the diaphragm?**<br>a) Flat shaped muscle with ligaments and tendons<br>b) A large dome shaped sheet of muscle<br>c) A large dome shaped muscle with a sheet of tendon with muscle fibres<br>d) U shaped muscle with muscle & nerve fibres<br><br>*Answer:* _____ | **56. Inflammation of the bronchial tubes is known as;**<br>a) Emphysema<br>b) Bronchitis<br>c) Pleurisy<br>d) Pneumonia<br><br><br><br><br><br>*Answer:* _____ |

| | |
|---|---|
| **57. What is the position of the pharyngeal tonsils?**<br>a) Under the palate<br>b) Back of the nose<br>c) Either side of the pharynx<br>d) Back of the larynx<br><br>*Answer:* _____ | **58. The voice box is also known as;**<br>a) Trachea<br>b) Larynx<br>c) Pharynx<br>d) Bronchi<br><br><br>*Answer:* _____ |
| **59. Which one of the following is a function of the pharynx?**<br>a) To neutralise bacteria<br>b) To carry air into the bronchioles<br>c) Helps to move food into the stomach<br>d) Lubricating the air passageways<br><br>*Answer:* _____ | **60. Which one of the following is not a function of the larynx?**<br>a) Helps in voice generation<br>b) Acts as a passageway for air<br>c) Act as a passageway for air between the pharynx and the bronchi<br>d) To prevent choking<br><br>*Answer:* _____ |
| **61. Where are the lungs positioned?**<br>a) Below the heart<br>b) Either side of the heart<br>c) Above the heart<br>d) Behind the heart<br><br>*Answer:* _____ | **62. Micturition is another term for;**<br>a) Expelling of urine<br>b) Faeces explusion<br>c) Exhalation<br>d) Giving birth<br><br>*Answer:* _____ |
| **63. Emphysema occurs when;**<br>a) The pleural lining becomes inflamed<br>b) The bronchi becomes inflamed<br>c) The oesophagus loses its elasticity<br>d) Alveolar walls are destroyed<br><br><br>*Answer:* _____ | **64. What is the respiratory centre in the medulla oblongata's role in breathing?**<br>a) Inhalation<br>b) To exhale<br>c) To stop inspiration<br>d) Relaxes the diaphragm<br><br>*Answer:* _____ |
| **65. Difficulty in exhaling is known as;**<br>a) Bronchitis<br>b) Emphysema<br>c) Pleurisy<br>d) Asthma<br><br>*Answer:* _____ | **66. Air travels from the larynx to;**<br>a) Trachea<br>b) Bronchi<br>c) Alveoli<br>d) Lungs<br><br>*Answer:* _____ |

| 67. The passage of air is as follows; | 68. Rhinitis is a term for; |
|---|---|
| a) Nose, pharynx, larynx, trachea, bronchioles, bronchi<br>b) Bronchioles, alveoli, larynx, trachea<br>c) Nose, larynx, pharynx, trachea, alveoli, bronchi, lungs<br>d) Nose, pharynx, larynx, trachea, bronchi, bronchioles, alveoli, lungs<br><br>*Answer:* _____ | a) Swelling and itchy eyes<br>b) Allergies<br>c) Stuffy, blocked nose and sinus problems<br>d) Coughing and night sweats<br><br>*Answer:* _____ |
| **69. Inflammation of the sinuses is known as;**<br>a) Rhinitis<br>b) Hay fever<br>c) Sinusitis<br>d) Bronchitis<br><br>*Answer:* _____ | **70. What is the larynx made of?**<br>a) Cartilage<br>b) Fibrous tissue<br>c) Ligaments<br>d) Connective tissue<br><br>*Answer:* _____ |

# The Respiratory System - Crossword 1

## Across

1. Where in the lungs does the exchange of gases take place? (7)
4. What does the trachea branch off to form? (7)
8. The first passageway for air entering the body (4)
9. A serous membrane that surrounds the lungs (6)
11. Voice box (6)
12. Shortness of breath, difficulty in breathing (6)
13. A lobe of the lungs (8)
14. What is lung tissue partly made up of? (6)

## Down

2. Large organs situated either side of the heart (5)
3. Inflammation of the bronchial tubes (10)
5. What is the nose made up of? (9)
6. Inhalation (11)
7. Exchange of gases (9)
10. A passageway for air between the larynx and bronchi (7)

# The Respiratory System - Crossword 2

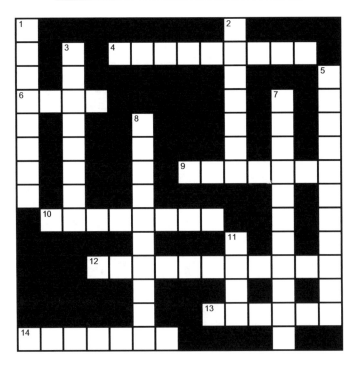

## Across

4. What muscle separates the chest from the abdominal cavity? (9)
6. An organ of smell (4)
9. What type of tissue are bronchioles partly made up of? (7)
10. Inflammation of the pleura (8)
12. Muscle between the ribs (11)
13. What type of membrane is the pleura? (6)
14. What type of cartilage is the trachea made of? (7)

## Down

1. Inflammation of the mucous membrane in the nose (8)
2. A continuation of the larynx (7)
3. Inner layer of the pleura (8)
5. An extension of the bronchi (11)
7. A body action which the diaphragm helps to control (11)
8. Exhalation (10)
11. What is the inside of the nose mostly made up of? (4)

# The Respiratory System – Crossword 3

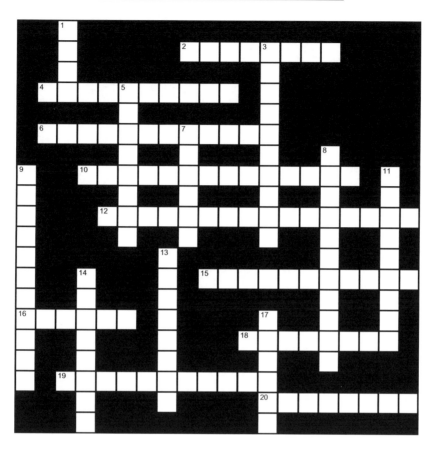

**Across**

2. What type of epithelium is the trachea lined with? (8)
4. What does the pharynx divide into, to allow the passage of food? (10)
6. A bacterial infection which often affects the lungs (12)
10. Nerve cells which stimulate the respiratory centre (14)
12. Air filled spaces within the bones surrounding the nose (16)
15. What body action does the diaphragm help with? (11)
16. What consists of the parietal and visceral layers? (6)
18. What does the larynx filter? (8)
19. A part of the brain involved in breathing (11)
20. A bronchiole at the end of the respiratory tract (8)

**Down**

1. What part of the respiratory system acts as a filter for dust and bacteria? (4)
3. What does the thyroid cartilage in the larynx form? (10)
5. Outer layer of the pleura (8)
7. What links the pharynx to the trachea? (6)
8. The smallest passageways of air (11)
9. What divides the left and right nasal cavities? (11)
11. Inflammation of the lung tissue (9)
13. What type of respiration describes the diffusion of oxygen from the blood into the cells and carbon dioxide from the cells into the bloodstream? (8)
14. What type of epithelium are alveoli made of? (8)
17. What is the space called between the visceral pleura and parietal pleura? (6)

## Multiple Choice Answers – The Respiratory System

| | | | | | | | | | |
|---|---|---|---|---|---|---|---|---|---|
| 1 | D | 21 | C | 41 | A | 61 | B |
| 2 | A | 22 | A | 42 | B | 62 | A |
| 3 | C | 23 | C | 43 | B | 63 | D |
| 4 | D | 24 | D | 44 | B | 64 | A |
| 5 | A | 25 | B | 45 | A | 65 | D |
| 6 | C | 26 | C | 46 | D | 66 | A |
| 7 | D | 27 | A | 47 | C | 67 | D |
| 8 | B | 28 | A | 48 | D | 68 | C |
| 9 | B | 29 | D | 49 | A | 69 | C |
| 10 | B | 30 | B | 50 | A | 70 | A |
| 11 | A | 31 | A | 51 | D | | |
| 12 | C | 32 | D | 52 | A | | |
| 13 | D | 33 | B | 53 | B | | |
| 14 | B | 34 | D | 54 | B | | |
| 15 | A | 35 | B | 55 | C | | |
| 16 | D | 36 | C | 56 | B | | |
| 17 | C | 37 | D | 57 | B | | |
| 18 | C | 38 | B | 58 | B | | |
| 19 | C | 39 | C | 59 | C | | |
| 20 | D | 40 | D | 60 | C | | |

## Crossword Answers – The Respiratory System

### Crossword 1

**Across**
1. Alveoli
4. Bronchi
8. Nose
9. Pleura
11. Larynx
12. Asthma
13. Superior
14. Nerves

**Down**
2. Lungs
3. Bronchitis
5. Cartilage
6. Inspiration
7. Breathing
10. Trachea

### Crossword 2

**Across**
4. Diaphragm
6. Nose
9. Elastic
10. Pleurisy
12. Intercostal
13. Serous
14. Hyaline

**Down**
1. Rhinitis
2. Trachea
3. Visceral
5. Bronchioles
7. Micturition
8. Expiration
11. Bone

## Crossword 3

| Across | Down |
|--------|------|
| 2. Ciliated | 1. Nose |
| 4. Oesophagus | 3. Adam's Apple |
| 6. Tuberculosis | 5. Parietal |
| 10. Chemoreceptors | 7. Larynx |
| 12. Paranasal Sinuses | 8. Bronchioles |
| 15. Parturition | 9. Nasal Septum |
| 16. Pleura | 11. Pneumonia |
| 18. Bacteria | 13. Internal |
| 19. Pons Varolii | 14. Squamous |
| 20. Terminal | 17. Cavity |

# Chapter 12 | The Urinary System

## Multiple Choice Questions

| | |
|---|---|
| **1. The hilium is a term for;**<br>a) The entrance of the kidney<br>b) The inside of the kidney<br>c) The membrane surrounding the kidney<br>d) The depression on the medial border of the kidney<br><br><br>*Answer:* _____ | **2. What is the function of the ureters?**<br>a) To transport urine from the bladder to the outside of the body<br>b) To collect urine from the urethra and pass it into the bladder<br>c) To store urine<br>d) To transport urine from the kidneys to the bladder<br><br>*Answer:* _____ |
| **3. What is kidney tissue made of?**<br>a) Fibrous tissue<br>b) Nephrons<br>c) Elastic tissue<br>d) Nerves and vessels<br><br>*Answer:* _____ | **4. How does blood enter the kidneys?**<br>a) Capillaries<br>b) Afferent arterioles<br>c) Efferent arterioles<br>d) Arteries<br><br>*Answer:* _____ |
| **5. What is the function of the bladder?**<br>a) To pass urine into the urether<br>b) To store urine<br>c) To reabsorb water back into the bloodstream<br>d) To collect urine from the ureter and pass it into the urethra<br><br>*Answer:* _____ | **6. Where does each kidney excrete urine?**<br>a) Renal pelvis<br>b) Bladder<br>c) Urethra<br>d) Ureter<br><br><br>*Answer:* _____ |
| **7. What is the main composition of urine?**<br>a) Urea<br>b) Salts<br>c) Water<br>d) Calcium<br><br>*Answer:* _____ | **8. Where is the bladder located?**<br>a) In the pelvic cavity<br>b) Outside the kidney<br>c) Above the kidney<br>d) Inside the kidney<br><br>*Answer:* _____ |

**9. What is the function of the Bowman's Capsule?**

a) Absorption of waste products

b) Acts as a passageway for urine through the kidneys

c) Acts as the first step for filtering blood in the kidneys

d) To carry waste products from the glomerulus to the loop of henle

*Answer:* _____

**10. What is the function of nephrons?**

a) Production of heat

b) Filtering bacteria from urine

c) Filtering the blood

d) Absorbing waste products

*Answer:* _____

**11. The muscular tubes which connect the kidneys to the bladder are;**

a) Ureters

b) Urethra

c) Renal pelvis

d) Hilium

*Answer:* _____

**12. Where is the medulla located?**

a) On the outside of the renal pelvis

b) On the inside of the kidney

c) On the inside of the renal pelvis

d) On the outside of the kidney

*Answer:* _____

**13. What acts as the first step in the filtration of blood to form urine?**

a) Bowman's capsule

b) Glomerulus

c) Nephron

d) Loop of henle

*Answer:* _____

**14. The loop of henle is an extension of;**

a) Distal convoluted tubules

b) Proximal convoluted tubules

c) Nephrons

d) Bowman's capsule

*Answer:* _____

**15. How does blood enter the kidney?**

a) Renal tubule

b) Efferent arteriole

c) Afferent arteriole

d) Renal artery

*Answer:* _____

**16. Nephritis is a term which describes;**

a) Inflammation of the bladder

b) Inflammation of the gall bladder

c) Inflammation of the kidney

d) Inflammation of the pelvis

*Answer:* _____

| | |
|---|---|
| **17. The cortex is located;**<br>a) On the inside of the kidney<br>b) Pelvis<br>c) On the outside of the kidney<br>d) Gall bladder<br><br><br>*Answer:* _____ | **18. What is the function of the renal pelvis?**<br>a) To filter the blood<br>b) To collect waste<br>c) To collect urine in the medulla and transport it into the ureter<br>d) To collect urine from the ureter and transport it into the urethra<br><br>*Answer:* _____ |
| **19. What sphincter controls the flow of urine through the urethra?**<br>a) Esophageal<br>b) External<br>c) Pyloric<br>d) Cardiac<br><br>*Answer:* _____ | **20. Urine passes from the bladder to;**<br>a) Ureters<br>b) Gall bladder<br>c) Urethra<br>d) Renal pelvis<br><br><br><br>*Answer:* _____ |
| **21. Inflammation of the bladder is known as;**<br>a) Kidney stones<br>b) Cystitis<br>c) Nephritis<br>d) Pleurisy<br><br><br><br><br><br><br><br><br>*Answer:* _____ | **22. What is the relationship between the urinary and circulatory systems?**<br>a) Reabsorption of oxygen and carbon dioxide from the blood takes place in the kidneys<br>b) The kidneys filter all the blood in the body<br>c) The chemical catalysts in the blood help with the filtration of urine in the kidneys<br>d) Erythrocytes in the blood help with the filtration of urine in the kidneys<br><br>*Answer:* _____ |
| **23. A hormone secreted by the kidneys;**<br>a) Renin<br>b) Oxytocin<br>c) Adrenaline<br>d) Melanin<br><br>*Answer:* _____ | **24. What is the renal pelvis?**<br>a) A bean shaped organ<br>b) A funnel shaped cavity<br>c) A sac like organ<br>d) A network of vessels<br><br>*Answer:* _____ |

| 25. Which of the following does not enter the hilium of the kidney?<br>a) Urethra<br>b) Renal vein<br>c) Renal artery<br>d) Renal pelvis<br><br>*Answer:* _____ | 26. How much urine is produced everyday?<br>a) 1.5 litres<br>b) 2 litres<br>c) 2.5 litres<br>d) 5 litres<br><br>*Answer:* _____ |
|---|---|
| 27. Filtered substances are passed from the bowman's capsule to;<br>a) Proximal convoluted tubules<br>b) Glomerular capsule<br>c) Renal pelvis<br>d) Cortex<br><br>*Answer:* _____ | 28. What is the function of the urethra?<br>a) To take urine from the bladder to outside the body<br>b) To store urine<br>c) To pass urine from the bladder to the ureter<br>d) To filter waste<br><br>*Answer:* _____ |
| 29. What is the structure of the bladder?<br>a) A funnel shaped organ<br>b) A funnel shaped cavity<br>c) A bean shaped organ<br>d) A hollow sac like organ<br><br>*Answer:* _____ | 30. Which one of the following is not a function of the kidney?<br>a) Urine production<br>b) Reabsorption of substances such as glucose and amino acids<br>c) Filtration of blood<br>d) Absorption of water<br><br>*Answer:* _____ |

## The Urinary System - Crossword 1

**Across**

1. The concave centre of the kidney (6)
5. Sphincter of the urethra which is voluntarily controlled by the central nervous system (8)
7. What substance does the kidney form? (5)
8. The outside part of the kidney (6)
9. Where is the bladder located? (12)
12. Where is urine stored? (7)
13. Filtration units found in the kidneys (8)
14. Inflammation of the bladder (8)

**Down**

2. What tube takes urine from the kidneys to the bladder? (6)
3. What connects the medulla to the ureter? (11)
4. The inside part of the kidney (7)
6. A narrow tube which leads from the bladder to the outside of the body (7)
10. Blood enters the kidneys via what type of arterioles (8)
11. A bean shaped organ which lies on the posterior wall of the abdomen (6)

# The Urinary System - Crossword 2

**Across**

4. A long loop which extends from the proximal convoluted tubules (11)
6. A substance found in urine (7)
7. Inflammation of the kidney (9)
9. Tubules that lead away from the Bowman's Capsule (8)
12. Tube that takes urine from inside the body to the outside of the body (7)
13. A muscular sac like organ in the pelvic cavity (7)
14. Deposits of substances found in urine (12)

**Down**

1. What collects urine from the renal pyramids in the medulla and passes it into the ureter (11)
2. Capillaries surrounded by the glomerular capsule (10)
3. Type of diabetes which causes excessive urine production (9)
5. Twisted tubules in the urinary system where filtered liquid is passed (10)
8. A bile pigment which gives urine its colour (9)
10. Where does reabsorption take place during urine production? (7)
11. Tubes which connect the kidneys to the bladder (7)

## Multiple Choice Answers – The Urinary System

| | | | | |
|----|---|---|----|---|
| 1 | D | | 21 | B |
| 2 | D | | 22 | B |
| 3 | B | | 23 | A |
| 4 | B | | 24 | B |
| 5 | B | | 25 | A |
| 6 | D | | 26 | A |
| 7 | C | | 27 | A |
| 8 | A | | 28 | A |
| 9 | C | | 29 | D |
| 10 | C | | 30 | D |
| 11 | A | | | |
| 12 | B | | | |
| 13 | A | | | |
| 14 | B | | | |
| 15 | D | | | |
| 16 | C | | | |
| 17 | C | | | |
| 18 | C | | | |
| 19 | B | | | |
| 20 | C | | | |

## Crossword Answers – The Urinary System

### Crossword 1

**Across**
1. Hilium
5. External
7. Urine
8. Cortex
9. Pelvic Cavity
12. Bladder
13. Nephrons
14. Cystitis

**Down**
2. Ureter
3. Renal Pelvis
4. Medulla
6. Urethra
10. Afferent
11. Kidney

### Crossword 2

**Across**
4. Loop of Henle
6. Ammonia
7. Nephritis
9. Proximal
12. Urethra
13. Bladder
14. Kidney Stones

**Down**
1. Renal Pelvis
2. Glomerulus
3. Insipidus
5. Convoluted
8. Bilirubin
10. Tubules
11. Ureters

# Chapter 13 | Revision Crosswords

## Anatomy & Physiology - Crossword 1

**Across**

2. Bone at the back of the skull (9)
7. A break in the walls of the alimentary tract (5)
8. A tube that acts as a passageway for urine from in the inside of the body to the outside? (7)
10. Cancer of the blood (9)
13. Facial paralysis (10)
17. Largest part of the brain (8)
18. Bone at the top of the arm (7)
19. Collar bone (8)
21. Vein of the arm (8)
23. A hormone secreted by the thyroid gland (10)
26. Skeletal muscle (9)
27. Endocrine gland in the thorax (6)
28. Moving muscle (7)
29. What part of the respiratory system prevents dust and bacteria from entering the lungs? (4)
30. A chronic inflammatory skin disorder (9)

---

**Down**

1. Where is bile stored before it reaches the duodenum? (11)
3. What is the majority of a cell made up of? (10)
4. Cell division (7)
5. Part of the urinary system that filters the blood (6)
6. Part of the small intestine (7)
9. A function of the tongue (10)
11. A function of the skin (10)
12. A composition of blood (6)
14. Turning the hand to face upwards (10)
15. Red blood cells (12)
16. What contains fluid and an immature ovum? (8)
20. White blood cells that engulf and digest bacteria and any harmful waste (10)
22. Stores and transports sperm (10)
24. A chemical messenger secreted directly into the bloodstream by a gland (7)
25. Where does the exchange of gases in the lungs take place? (7)

# Anatomy & Physiology - Crossword 2

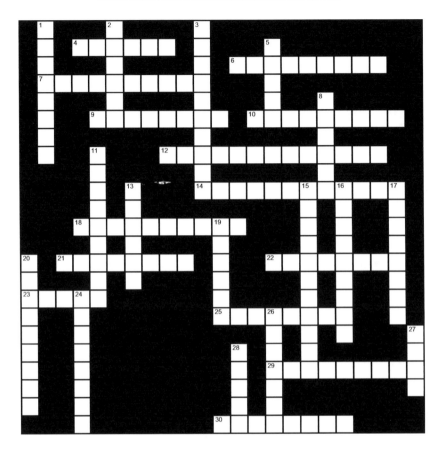

**Across**

4. A serous membrane on the outside of each lung (6)

6. What type of circulation travels from the heart to the lungs? (9)

7. Fibrous tissue which provides support for lymph nodes (10)

9. Main muscle of mastication (8)

10. A type of muscle contraction (9)

12. A type of connective tissue which allows stretching of various organs (13)

14. Power houses of the cell (12)

18. A plasma protein (10)

21. Muscle which flexes the knee (8)

22. Sweat glands which excrete a milky substance (8)

23. Lack of muscle tone (5)

25. What phase of mitosis do the chromatids separate and become chromosomes? (8)

29. Hormone secreted by the ovaries (9)

30. Lower jaw bone (8)

**Down**

1. Inflammation of the bladder (8)
2. Swelling in the body tissues (6)
3. Part of the brain which co-ordinates muscular activity (10)
5. Tip of the penis (5)
8. An enzyme that breaks proteins down into polypeptides (6)
11. Gland situated in the base of the brain (9)
13. Neck of the uterus (6)
15. What type of cells is bone tissue made of? (11)
16. Nerve fibres which carry the nerve impulses towards the cell body (9)
17. A loss of appetite (8)
19. A skin condition featuring dry, itchy patches with small blisters that may weep when scratched (6)
20. When the heart is relaxing (9)
24. Inflammation of a nerve (8)
26. A salivary gland (7)
27. Bones that allow movement (4)
28. Whiteheads (5)

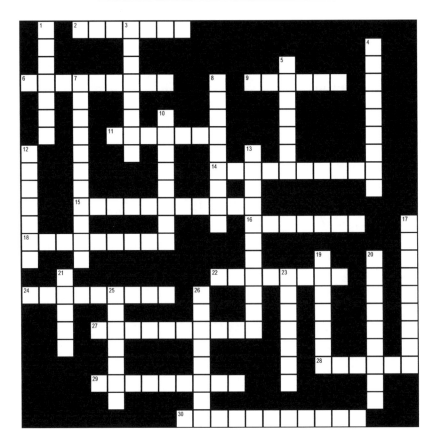

## Across

2. What part of the digestive system commences the digestion of proteins? (7)
6. External respiration (9)
9. What muscle plantarflexes the foot? (6)
11. A substance produced in the liver (7)
14. Hormone secreted by the adrenal medulla (10)
15. Low blood pressure (11)
16. Artery of the head and neck (7)
18. Freckles (9)
22. What nerves supply the chest muscles? (8)
24. Inflammation of the lung tissue (9)
27. A type of bone tissue found at the ends of long bones that has a spongy appearance (10)
28. Muscular wall which separates the left and right side of the heart (6)
29. A phase of the menstrual cycle (9)
30. What is the spleen responsible for producing? (11)

**Down**

1. Breast bone (7)
3. A connective tissue which protects the whole of the central nervous system (8)
4. What part of the cell manufactures proteins? (9)
5. Bending a body part so there is a decrease in the angle between the bones (7)
7. Absence of menstruation (11)
8. What muscle moves the scalp forwards? (9)
10. What endocrine gland produces insulin and glucagon? (8)
12. A sac that stores urine (7)
13. What do bronchi divide into? (11)
17. Tail of the sperm (9)
19. A type of connective tissue (7)
20. Inflammation of a vein (9)
21. Thigh bone (5)
23. An enzyme contained within pancreatic juice (7)
25. Female gonads (7)
26. Part of a neuron (8)

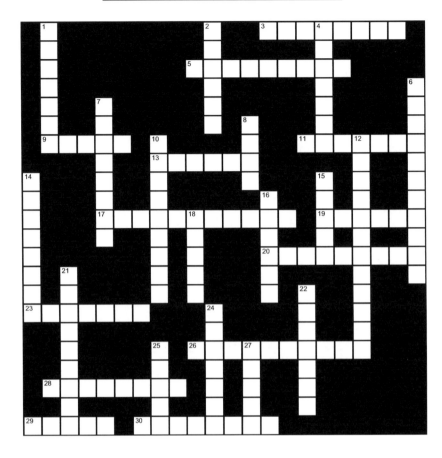

## Across

3. The start of menstruation (8)
5. Hives (9)
9. Substance that keeps the skin moist (5)
11. Shoulder muscle (7)
13. The fixed end of a muscle (6)
17. Smallest blood vessels (11)
19. Lower back (6)
20. Hormone secreted by the pineal body (9)
23. Afferent nodes (7)
26. Lower chambers of the heart (10)
28. What part of the brain is found between the cerebrum and cerebellum? (8)
29. Male organ of reproduction (5)
30. Inflammation of the pleura (8)

**Down**

1. Part of the cell that controls the cell's activities (7)
2. Outer part of the kidney (6)
4. Fatty tissue (7)
6. Tubes leading from the epididymis to the urethra, acting as a passageway for sperm (11)
7. Excessive bile pigments in the blood, causing a yellowing of the skin (8)
8. What type of bone is the radius (4)
10. Lymph nodes located behind the knee (9)
12. Cells responsible for blood clotting (12)
14. Muscle which creates a grinning expression (8)
15. External organs of the female reproductive system (5)
16. The deeper layer of the skin (6)
18. What carries excess waste away from the tissues? (5)
21. A function of the skin (9)
22. Part of the respiratory system that connects the larynx with the bronchi (7)
24. Most widely distributed connective tissue found on the body (7)
25. Part of the skeleton that supports the skull, neck and trunk (5)
27. What is the main weight bearing bone of the foot? (5)

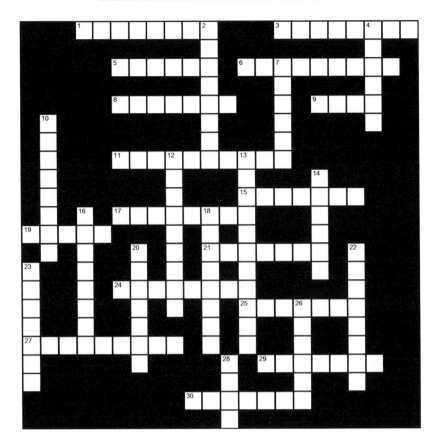

**Across**

1. Filtration units found in the kidneys (8)

3. A pigmentation disorder (8)

5. Male gonads (6)

6. The moving part of a muscle (9)

8. What do capillaries join up to form? (7)

9. Produced by the liver (4)

11. A function of the skin (11)

15. An enzyme produced by the pancreas (7)

17. At what stage of mitosis do the centrioles move toward each end of the cell and form spindles? (8)

19. Lower leg bone (5)

21. Part of an innominate bone (7)

24. Empty gaps within the cytoplasm (8)

25. Glands positioned in the neck (7)

27. Turning the hand to face downwards (9)

29. A substance which gives skin its colour (7)

30. After the nose, where does the air travel to? (7)

## Down

2. The transport of blood from the heart to the body (8)
4. Involuntary muscle (6)
7. A lymphatic organ (6)
10. Hormone responsible for the contraction of the uterus during labour (8)
12. A muscle covering the upper back (9)
13. Muscle positioned between the ribs (11)
14. Difficulty in breathing (6)
16. Part of the brain stem (8)
18. Nodes positioned in the armpits (8)
20. Mature follicles (8)
22. An exaggerated inward lower spine (8)
23. The point where nerve impulses pass from one neuron to the next neuron (7)
26. An automatic movement in response to a sensory stimulus (6)
28. What type of bone is the vomer? (4)

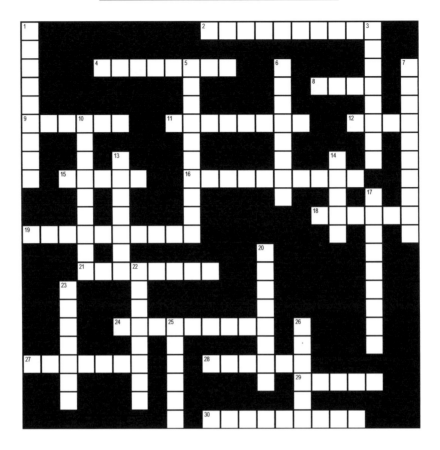

**Across**

2. During cell division what divides in 2 and moves to the opposite sides of the cell? (10)
4. Pigmentation disorder (8)
8. What breaks down fats into smaller droplets? (4)
9. What do a group of cells join to form? (6)
11. What does the nose filter? (8)
12. Infection around a hair follicle (4)
15. Folds of the stomach (5)
16. What muscle raises the lower jaw? (10)
18. The protrusion of an organ through the surface of a bodily structure (6)
19. Function of the pelvic girdle (10)
21. Bones that develop within tendons (8)
24. Part of the vulva (9)
27. A type of cartilage (7)
28. Central fissure of the kidney (6)
29. Thickest section of the muscle (5)
30. What muscle separates the chest cavity and the abdominal cavity? (9)

**Down**

1. The cerebrum controls what type of movement? (9)
3. Bone that forms the base of the skull (8)
5. Inspiration (10)
6. Wrist bone (8)
7. Salivary gland (10)
10. Inflammation of the sinuses (9)
13. Branches of the pelvis of the kidney (7)
14. Fibrous joints (5)
17. A ductless gland that secretes hormones (9)
20. Part of the penis (8)
22. What muscle is positioned at the elbow? 8)
23. Layer of the skin where desquamation takes place (7)
25. What phase of mitosis is the metaphase? (6)
26. Which plexus supplies the lower abdominal wall? (6)

## Anatomy & Physiology - Crossword 7

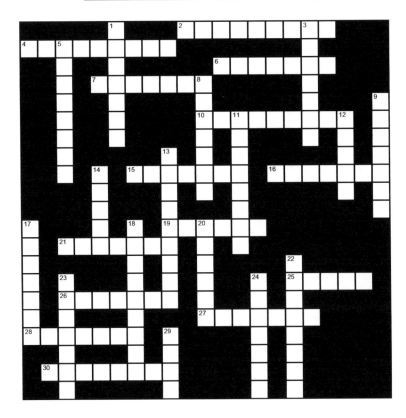

**Across**

2. Study of cells and tissues (9)

4. Cheek bones (9)

6. Vein of the arm (7)

7. A structure at the bottom of the hair follicle (7)

10. Blackheads (9)

15. What is the outer layer of lymphatic vessels made up of? (7)

16. Category of skin disorder (7)

19. A tarsal (6)

21. The point at which a neuron passes information to the next neuron (7)

25. Largest artery in the body (5)

26. A protein in the skin that allows skin to resume its shape after it is stretched or pulled (7)

27. A sac containing the testicles (7)

28. A function of the liver (7)

30. What part of the meninges surrounds the brain and spinal cord? (8)

## Down

1. Muscle which constricts and flares the nostrils (7)
3. Least moveable synovial joint (7)
5. A plasma protein (8)
8. What substance does the stomach absorb? (7)
9. Adrenal gland that responds to nervous impulses in the sympathetic nervous system (7)
11. Inflammation of a muscle (8)
12. What type of bone are the tarsals? (5)
13. Moving a limb away from the body (9)
14. What is the only bone in the human skeleton not articulated to any other bone? (5)
17. Muscular tubes which move urine from the kidneys to the bladder (7)
18. Cardiac cycle (9)
20. What muscle supinates the forearm? (6)
22. A storage cavity within the cytoplasm (8)
23. Reproduction of sex cells (7)
24. Branches of the respiratory tube that conduct air in and out of the lungs (7)
29. A viral infection often found on fingers (4)

## Across

1. What organs are enclosed within the rib cage? (5)
6. The second stage of mitosis (9)
9. Function of the skeleton (7)
10. An enzyme found in intestinal juice (7)
12. Duct which collects and drains lymph from the legs (8)
16. What part of the body does the vastus medialis extend? (4)
17. What part of the female reproductive system extends from the cervix to the vulva? (6)
18. Part of the brain that controls memory (8)
21. What does mitochondria supply the cell with? (6)
22. Bones with broad surfaces for muscle attachment (4)
25. Birthmark (6)
27. Where does digestion start? (5)
28. Type of connective tissue (8)
29. Turning the foot towards the centre (9)
30. Function of the skin (9)

**Down**

2. Lower arm bone (4)
3. Voluntary branch of the peripheral nervous system (7)
4. Thyrotrophin is secreted by what gland? (9)
5. Type of cells that destroy and digest harmful micro organisms (10)
7. Pressure felt in the arteries (5)
8. Type of circulation which transports blood between the heart and lungs (9)
11. Found in haversian canals (6)
13. Location of the pectoralis major (5)
14. Bones in the neck (8)
15. What type of infection is herpes simplex? (5)
19. Balance in the body (11)
20. A substance that helps to create a blood clot (6)
23. What connects muscle to bone? (6)
24. Efferent neurones (5)
26. How is the direction of blood maintained? (6)

**Across**

4. The rounded end of a long bone (9)
6. The active growth phase of hair follicles (6)
7. What muscle laterally flexes the trunk? (17)
11. What is the fold of skin in front of the cuticle? (6)
12. Infestation disorder (18)
14. Muscle found at the front of the neck (8)
15. A basic unit of matter (4)
17. Sole of the foot (7)
18. Anatomical plane which separates the left side of the body from the right (8)
19. A process whereby cells engulf and absorb liquids (11)
20. What is the skin called at the base of the fingernail? (7)

**Down**

1. Inflammation of the gums (10)
2. An enlarged lymphatic vessel at the lower end of the thoracic duct (13)
3. Nail disorder in which the skin adheres to the nail plate and grows forward as the nail grows out (9)
5. Nearest to the point of attachment to the body (8)
8. Patches of lymphoid tissue located in the wall of the small intestine (13)
9. Severe nail biting (11)
10. The process of bone formation (12)
13. Inflammation of the larynx (10)
16. Fine, non pigmented hair found on most of the body (6)

## Revision Crossword Answers

### Anatomy & Physiology – Crossword 1

**Across**
2. Occipital
7. Ulcer
8. Urethra
10. Leukaemia
13. Bell's Palsy
17. Cerebrum
18. Humerus
19. Clavicle
21. Cephalic
23. Calcitonin
26. Voluntary
27. Thymus
28. Agonist
29. Nose
30. Psoriasis

**Down**
1. Gall Bladder
3. Protoplasm
4. Mitosis
5. Kidney
6. Jejunum
9. Swallowing
11. Absorption
12. Plasma
14. Supination
15. Erythrocytes
16. Follicle
20. Phagocytes
22. Epididymis
24. Hormone
25. Alveoli

### Anatomy & Physiology – Crossword 2

**Across**
4. Pleura
6. Pulmonary
7. Trabeculae
9. Masseter
10. Isometric
12. Yellow Elastic
14. Mitochondria
18. Fibrinogen
21. Gracilis
22. Apocrine
23. Atony
25. Anaphase
29. Oestrogen
30. Mandible

**Down**
1. Cystitis
2. Oedema
3. Cerebellum
8. Pepsin
11. Pituitary
13. Cervix
15. Osteoblasts
16. Dendrites
17. Anorexia
19. Eczema
20. Diastolic
24. Neuritis
26. Parotid
27. Long
28. Milia

### Anatomy & Physiology – Crossword 3

**Across**
2. Stomach
6. Breathing
9. Soleus
11. Heparin
14. Adrenaline
15. Hypotension
16. Carotid
18. Ephelides
22. Thoracic
24. Pneumonia
27. Cancellous
28. Septum
29. Secretory
30. Lymphocytes

**Down**
1. Sternum
3. Meninges
4. Ribosomes
5. Flexion
7. Amenorrhoea
8. Frontalis
10. Pancreas
12. Bladder
13. Bronchioles
17. Flagellum
19. Fibrous
20. Phlebitis
21. Femur
23. Amylase
25. Ovaries
26. Cell Body

### Anatomy & Physiology – Crossword 4

**Across**
3. Menarche
5. Urticaria
9. Sebum
11. Deltoid
13. Origin
17. Capillaries
19. Lumbar
20. Melatonin
23. Sensory
26. Ventricles
28. Midbrain
29. Penis
30. Pleurisy

**Down**
1. Nucleus
2. Cortex
4. Adipose
6. Vas Deferens
7. Jaundice
8. Long
10. Popliteal
12. Thrombocytes
14. Risorius
15. Vulva
16. Dermis
18. Lymph
21. Sensation
22. Trachea
24. Areolar
25. Axial
27. Talus

## Anatomy & Physiology – Crossword 5

**Across**
1 Nephrons
3. Chloasma
5. Testes
6. Insertion
8. Venules
9. Heat
11. Protection
15. Trypsin
17. Prophase
19. Tibia
21. Ischium
24. Vacuoles
25. Thyroid
27. Pronation
29. Melanin
30. Pharynx

**Down**
2. Systemic
4. Smooth
7. Spleen
10. Oxytocin
12. Trapezius
13. Intercostal
14. Asthma
16. Midbrain
18. Axillary
20. Graafian
22. Lordosis
23. Synapse
26. Reflex
28. Flat

## Anatomy & Physiology – Crossword 6

**Across**
2. Centrioles
4. Vitiligo
8. Bile
9. Tissue
11. Bacteria
12. Boil
15. Rugae
16. Temporalis
18. Hernia
19. Protection
21. Sesamoid
24. Mons Pubis
27. Hyaline
28. Hilium
29. Belly
30. Diaphragm

**Down**
1. Voluntary
3. Sphenoid
5. Inhalation
6. Pisiform
7. Sublingual
10. Sinusitis
13. Calyces
14. Fixed
17. Endocrine
20. Foreskin
22. Anconeus
23. Surface
25. Second
26. Lumbar

## Anatomy & Physiology – Crossword 7

**Across**
2. Histology
4. Zygomatic
6. Basilic
7. Papilla
10. Comedones
15. Fibrous
16. General
19. Cuboid
21. End Feet
25. Aorta
26. Elastin
27. Scrotum
28. Storage
30. Pia Mater

**Down**
1. Nasalis
3. Gliding
5. Globulin
8. Alcohol
9. Medulla
11. Myositis
12. Short
13. Abduction
14. Hyoid
17. Ureters
18. Heartbeat
20. Biceps
22. Vacuoles
23. Meiosis
24. Bronchi
29. Wart

## Anatomy & Physiology – Crossword 8

**Across**
1. Lungs
6. Metaphase
9. Support
10. Lactase
12. Thoracic
16. Knee
17. Vagina
18. Cerebrum
21. Energy
22. Flat
25. Naevae
27. Mouth
28. Lymphoid
29. Inversion
30. Secretion

**Down**
2. Ulna
3. Somatic
4. Pituitary
5. Leucocytes
7. Pulse
8. Pulmonary
11. Nerves
13. Chest
14. Cervical
15. Viral
19. Homeostasis
20. Fibrin
23. Tendon
24. Motor
26. Valves

## Anatomy & Physiology – Crossword 9

**Across**

4. Epiphysis
6. Anagen
7. Quadratus Lumborum
11. Mantle
12. Pediculosis Capitis
14. Platysma
15. Atom
17. Plantar
18. Sagittal
19. Pinocytosis
20. Cuticle

**Down**

1. Gingivitis
2. Cisterna Chyli
3. Pterygium
5. Proximal
8. Peyers Patches
9. Onychophagy
10. Ossification
13. Laryngitis
16. Vellus

Made in the USA
San Bernardino, CA
07 March 2016